SPORT
SPEED

SPORT
SPEED

George B. Dintiman, EdD
Virginia Commonwealth University

Robert D. Ward, PED
Dallas Cowboy Football Club

Cofounders of the National Association for Speed and Explosion

Leisure Press

To those past, present, and future individuals who believe there are no limits to an athlete's accomplishments.

Library of Congress Cataloging-in-Publication Data

Dintiman, George B.
    Sportspeed / George B. Dintiman, Robert D. Ward
        p.   cm.
    ISBN 0-88011-325-1   (pbk.)
    1. Physical education and training. 2. Sprinting. 3. Speed.
    I. Ward, Robert D., 1933–   . II. Title.
    GV711.5.D56   1988
    613.7'07—dc19   88-4193
                                                                        CIP

Developmental Editor: June I. Decker, PhD; Copy Editor: Bruce Owens;
Assistant Editor: JoAnne Cline; Production Director: Ernie Noa;
Projects Manager: Lezli Harris; Typesetter: Sonnie Bowman; Text Design:
Keith Blomberg; Text Layout: Chris Terrell; Cover Design: Jack Davis;
Cover Photo: Rick Stewart/Focus West; Illustrations By: Mary Yemma Long;
Printed By: Versa Press

ISBN: 0-88011-325-1

Copyright © 1988 by George B. Dintiman and Robert D. Ward

Printed in the United States of America   10 9 8 7 6 5

Leisure Press
A Division of Human Kinetics Publishers
P.O. Box 5076, Champaign, IL 61825-5076
1-800-747-4457

Canada: Human Kinetics Publishers, P.O. Box 24040, Windsor, ON N8Y 4Y9
1-800-465-7301 (in Canada only)

Europe: Human Kinetics Publishers (Europe) Ltd., P.O. Box IW14,
Leeds LS16 6TR, England
0532-781708

Australia: Human Kinetics Publishers, P.O. Box 80, Kingswood 5062,
South Australia
618-374-0433

New Zealand: Human Kinetics Publishers, P.O. Box 105-231, Auckland 1
(09) 309-2259

Contents

Foreword

Speed has been the most important factor in my success as an athlete in football and track. It is also the single most important quality for achieving stardom in almost every sport. Interestingly, most coaches and athletes in the past have felt it was impossible to improve an athlete's speed to any great extent. Therefore, when I was competing, none of the highly technical methods for speed improvement were available. Although one can't relive the past, one question has crossed my mind many times: How fast could I have been? Calculations were made comparing my speed to speed-improvement data of other scientifically trained runners. Those calculations showed that a race among Ben Johnson (world record holder in the 100-meter dash at 9.83 seconds), Carl Lewis, and me would undoubtedly be the race of the century and would surely produce a world record time.

Modern-day athletes have the advantage of new techniques and new information on speed improvement. The authors of *Sportspeed*, George Dintiman and Bob Ward, are undoubtedly the two most knowledgeable people in the United States, perhaps in the world, in speed improvement for athletes in all sports. I am convinced that I would have benefited greatly from their 7-Step Model for speed improvement and become a much faster, much better athlete. On behalf of all those great runners and athletes of the past, I urge you, the runners and athletes of the present and future, to read and apply the training methods in *Sportspeed*.

Bob Hayes
former Olympic gold medal winner
NFL all-pro
and Dallas Cowboy

Acknowledgments

> *No individual (player-coach) has sufficient experience, education, native ability and knowledge to insure the accumulation of a great fortune without the cooperation of other people.*
> —Napoleon Hill
> **Think and Grow Rich**

The authors are indebted to the following individuals for their valuable assistance with the manuscript:

Bill Bates, Tony Dorsett, and Randy White of the Dallas Cowboys; Craig Reynolds and Nolan Ryan of the Houston Astros; and John MacLoed and Derek Harper of the Dallas Mavericks for sharing their training secrets; Ralph Mann, Larry Brown, and Steve Davison for helping us apply their innovative techniques and machinery to our speed improvement program;

Dr. Phil Osborne, MD, and Ed Kozak, brilliant musician and inventor of the motorvator computer game, for their insight into rhythm in sportspeed development.

Gene Coleman of the Houston Astros for his assistance with the speed improvement program for baseball players;

Lynne R. Mohn, MS, for the preparation of the very useful stride-rate matrix, the preparation of materials on the female athlete, and the editorial review of the entire manuscript;

Brenda Dintiman-Shanahan, MD, for her assistance with the medical aspects of the text;

Keith Wheeler, PhD, for the preparation of the chapter on sports nutrition;

the entire Dallas Cowboy organization for its cooperation with facilities, equipment, and photos; and a special note of appreciation to G. Brian Dintiman for holding the family business together in critical times while his father concentrated on speed improvement clinics, camps, symposia, and books.

Sportspeed is the result of over 25 years of work with team-sport athletes to improve their speed in short distances. The 7-Step Model for speed improvement was developed only after many years of experimentation and training with athletes of all ages, from Little League to the pros. This model is now used throughout the world by high school, college, and professional coaches in football, basketball, and baseball. The exciting part is that the model works. You can improve your speed in the 40-yard dash, for example, by as much as .9 seconds. Many athletes who attended our speed clinics and camps from 1972 to 1988 showed dramatic improvement in their speed and are now playing professional sports.

This book describes a step-by-step program that anyone can follow to improve speed. It is one of the most well researched and practical books on speed improvement. Everything you need to do, from completing five simple tests that locate your weaknesses to performing each step in the 7-Step Model, is presented in an easy-to-read style. More important, *you can do it alone and make yourself faster.* There is no need to train with a partner unless you want to.

Everything you ever wanted to know about sprinting faster for your sport is presented in this book. You can test, evaluate, and train yourself all in one summer. Sample workouts are presented that tell you exactly what to do, and a record system is included so you can chart your progress.

A chapter on sports nutrition clearly describes how you can achieve high energy for better game and practice performance, gain lean body weight and muscle, and lose fat weight.

This program cannot miss. Ask Bill Bates of the Dallas Cowboys or Carl Bland of the Detroit Lions. We cannot make it any easier—the rest is up to you. You can improve your speed with this book. It may be the most important book you ever read.

George B. Dintiman
Richmond, VA

Bob Ward
Dallas, TX

Chapter 1

Introduction

> To be what we are, and to become what we are capable of becoming is the only end of life.
> —Robert Louis Stevenson

Speed is the most important quality that an athlete can possess. This became evident to me as a high school football and track coach in southern California in the 1960s. One player who was not fond of hard contact, as either a running back or a defensive back, always amazed the coaching staff with his blinding speed and his ability to avoid tacklers and perfectly time his pass coverage. That year, his speed helped us win a conference championship. After graduation, it enabled him to become an outstanding receiver at the University of Southern California. Speed can overcome a number of other weaknesses in football, basketball, and baseball, allowing one to perform at extremely high levels of competition.

The importance of speed can also be illustrated by the example of the fragile straw overcoming the mighty oak. The straw uses the tremendous wind speeds of the tornado to develop the force needed to pierce the hard oak tree. Athletes with superior speed also can make up for lack of size and weight and often can overpower stronger, heavier players.

Get ready to sprint faster because, if you use the speed improvement program described in this book, that is exactly what will happen, just as it happened to all-pro Bill Bates, who came to the Dallas Cowboys running the 40-yard dash in 4.79 seconds, then in 1986 ran it in 4.59 seconds. This amazing improvement shows what can be done if the desire to sprint faster is combined with proper speed training. You can improve your sprinting speed even more and in a shorter period of time than Bill did if you believe that you can sprint faster and apply the 7-Step Model to your training program. This can be your shortcut to athletic success. While other athletes follow a trial-and-error method, you will be systematically working on a total speed improvement program, the same program that many outstanding professional and amateur athletes have used to improve their speed. This approach has been condensed into a "can't-miss" model for developing speed that includes seven essential steps; therefore, it has been named the 7-Step Model. Many Dallas Cowboy players have improved their 40-yard-dash times by as much as .2 seconds. Older professional players have also been able to maintain or regain lost speed, thereby extending the length and the quality of their careers. Carl Bland, a wide receiver with the Detroit Lions, entered a speed camp and followed the 7-Step Model for more than a year, improving his speed enough not only to make the squad but to earn himself a starting role. High school and college athletes in basketball, baseball, and football have bettered their times by as much as .7 seconds.

Football teams in the past have had the advantage of fielding outstanding players with great speed, but only the Dallas Cowboys can put two of the fastest, most explosive backs ever to play the game on the field at the same time. Their collective speed would impress some of the "dynamic duos" of football fame. Army's Glenn B.

Figure 1.1 Tony Dorsett is one of fastest most explosive players in NFL history.

Davis and Doc D. Blanchard, for example, had different gifts: Davis was known for his speed and Blanchard for his sheer running power. Many teams have one speedster, but few can boast of two backs with blinding acceleration, power, and speed. Tony Dorsett (Figure 1.1) could be considered the straw that overcame the mighty oak, but Herschel Walker is the mighty oak who can leap tall buildings almost in a single bound and stop locomotives. In track and field, Herschel has recorded times that rank him as a world-class sprinter. Had Tony been a track athlete, he likely would have reached the world-class level.

Not all professional football players have blinding speed. In fact, some athletes can do no better than a 5.4 or 5.5 in the 40-yard dash. You can be a great athlete and still not be as fast and quick as Tony Dorsett or Herschel Walker, Michael Jordan of professional basketball fame, or Bo Jackson and Willie Wilson of the Kansas City Royals. You do not need to have the quickest first step in basketball (Figure 1.3) or be the league leader in stolen bases (Figure 1.3). The key is to become as fast as your potential allows. You can reach your potential only by following a holistic program such as the 7-Step Model. You must make the commitment to become faster. Otherwise, you'll become an extremely fit athlete who continually gets beaten.

Figure 1.2 Speed and explosive training can improve the leaping ability of any basketball player.

Figure 1.3 Speed and explosiveness are a dangerous combination for a baserunner.

Great teams have not only well-oiled offensive machines but also great defensive power. Two other Cowboys have made a tremendous impact on professional football. Who has not heard of the "Manster" (half man and half monster), Randy White the incomparable all-pro defensive tackle whose mere shadow is enough to send chills down the spines of running backs. If Randy does not get you, all-pro Ed "Too Tall" Jones will.

How do superior players train to achieve such uncommon results? They spend hour after hour increasing their basic fitness levels, which include body control, power, strength, cardioaerobics, and speed. They build the skills required for their positions on this foundation of basic fitness.

Success did not come easily for the Herschel Walkers, Tony Dorsetts, Magic Johnsons, and Brooks Robinsons of the sports world, and it will not come easily to you. However, if you follow the 7-Step Model to success, you could develop more strength, power, and speed than you ever dreamed possible.

We know you are anxious to get to that "can't-miss stairway" to sport speed—the 7-Step Model. But first we will cover some simple tests to give you an idea of where you are now so that we can help you plan your program to faster speed. Remember that the future belongs to those who prepare, so go for it!

Chapter 2

Getting Started

Nothing great was ever achieved without enthusiasm.

—Ralph Waldo Emerson

Your first step toward increasing your sport speed is to work with a friend or coach and test yourself on five factors: a stationary 120-yard dash, leg strength, hamstring/quadricep strength, stride length, and a future 40-yard dash. Although other tests could be conducted, these five give you all the information you need. Try to be accurate when scoring each factor. The more accurate the test scores, the more successful your speed improvement program will be. Test standards apply to both male and female athletes unless otherwise indicated. Once you know your strengths and weaknesses, it is easier to concentrate on the workout programs that will make a difference for you in your sport.

Stationary 120-Yard Dash

Use a track or a three-point football stance (Figure 2.1) on a track or a grass area and begin your sprint whenever you are ready. Be sure to sprint at full speed for the entire 120 yards.

Place a timer at the 40-, 80-, and 120-yard marks (finish line). Stretch a finish cord, with a handkerchief or flag draped over it, at the 40-, 80-, and 120-yard marks. Timer 1 stands at the 40-yard mark, starts a stopwatch on your first movement, and stops it when the flag on the tape at the 40-yard mark moves. Timer 2 stands at the 80-yard mark, starts a stopwatch when the flag at the 40-yard mark moves, and stops it when the flag at the 80-yard mark moves. Timer 3 starts a stopwatch when the flag at the 80-yard mark moves and stops it when the flag at the finish line moves.

Figure 2.1 Start of the 120-yard dash.

On your test score sheet (Table 2.1), record your 40-yard time to the right of "Stationary 40," your time from the 40-yard mark to the 80-yard mark next to "Flying 40," and your time from the 80-yard to the 120-yard mark to the right of "80–120-yard time." Your *speed endurance score* is the difference between your flying 40-yard time and your 80–120-yard time.

After one 120-yard sprint, you already know a lot about yourself and can now evaluate your 40-yard-dash time as well as your speed endurance. Additional information from this 120-yard sprint will be used later.

40-Yard-Dash Time

Remember that everyone can improve 40-yard-dash time, and no matter what your time was, it will improve with training. Even in professional football, not everyone is superfast. Speed is important, but you do not have to be as fast as Tony Dorsett to be a star. The same is true in basketball and baseball. Larry Bird is not the quickest or the fastest player in the National Basketball Association, but he overcomes this weakness with tremendous skill and determination. Gerald Perry of the Atlanta Braves and Rickey Henderson of the New York Yankees also lack blinding speed, but they are two of the best base runners and base stealers, respectively, in professional baseball. With proper training, Bird, Perry, and Henderson could become much quicker and faster, and so can you.

Table 2.1 Test Score Sheet

Test	Score	Standard	Weakness?	Programs in the 7-Step Model
1. 120-yard dash Stationary 40 Flying 40 Speed endurance:	— — — —	No more than .1 sec between fly-ing 40- and 80–120-yd time	— Yes — No	☐ Basic training ☐ Functional strength/power ☐ Sporting speed/speed endurance
80–120-yd time Difference between flying 40 and 80–120-yd time	—			
2. Leg strength Leg press	—	Multiply body weight by 2.5 (your score should be higher)	— Yes — No	☐ Basic training ☐ Functional strength/power ☐ Sprint loading
3. Hamstring/quadricep strength Leg curl Leg extension Leg curl ÷ leg extension	— — —	Hamstring strength (leg curl) should be at least 75% of quadri-cep strength (leg extension)	— Yes — No	☐ Basic training ☐ Functional strength/power ☐ Sprint loading

(Cont.)

Table 2.1 (Cont.)

Test	Score	Standard	Weakness?	Programs in the 7-Step Model
4. Stride length	_____	Find your range from the stride-length matrix (Table 2.2)	Yes _____ No _____	☐ Plyometrics ☐ Sporting speed ☐ Overspeed
5. NASE future-40 test	_____	This score provides an estimate of your potential for improvement. Add .3 sec to this score before subtracting it from your stationary 40-yd time. This is your potential for improvement.		
Stride rate	_____	Use Table 2.3 to find your ideal stride rate	Yes _____ No _____	☐ Overspeed
Acceleration Stationary 40 Flying 40 Acceleration time (stationary 40 – flying 40)	_____ _____ _____	No more than a .7 sec difference	Yes _____ No _____	☐ Ballistics ☐ Sprint loading ☐ Sporting speed

Speed Endurance

This score compares your flying 40-yard time (40–80-yard-dash time) to your 80–120-yard-dash time. If both scores are the same, or almost so, you are in excellent physical condition to sprint a short distance such as 40 yards repeatedly during a football, basketball, or baseball game without slowing down due to fatigue. If your flying 40-yard time and your 80–120-yard time (also a flying 40) differ by more than .1 seconds, check the program "Sporting speed/speed endurance" on your test score sheet. The program will improve your speed endurance.

Leg Strength

Adjust the seat on a Universal, Nautilus, or similar leg press station until your legs are at right angles. Find the amount of weight you can press for only one repetition. On your first attempt, try to press an amount of weight equal to 2 times your body weight. If that amount is too much or too little, rest 3 minutes and add or remove weight before trying again. Continue to add or remove weight until you locate the amount, to the nearest 10 pounds, that you can press only once (Figure 2.2). Record this amount to the right of "Leg press" on your test score sheet.

Figure 2.2 Leg press.

You should be able to press 2.5 times your body weight. For example, if you weigh 150 pounds, your leg press score should be at least 375 pounds (150 × 2.5 = 375). If your score is less than 2.5 times your body weight, check the program "Functional strength/power training" on your test score sheet. You need to increase your leg strength.

Hamstring/Quadricep Strength

Using a Universal, Nautilus, or similar leg extension/leg curl station, find the amount of weight that you can extend and curl only once. Sit erect at the end of the station with your hands grasping the sides of the seat. Connect both feet under the leg press pad and try to extend your legs. Use the same procedure described above for adding and removing weight until you find the amount of weight you can move just once. Now lie on your stomach, connect your heels to the leg curl pad, grasp the sides of the seat with both hands, and flex both legs to your buttocks (Figure 2.3 a, b). Record these scores to the right of "Leg extension" and "Leg curl" on your test score sheet.

Ideally, your leg extension (quadricep muscle group) and leg curl (hamstring muscle group) scores should be the same. However, in almost every athlete at all ages the quadricep muscles (leg press) are much stronger than the hamstring muscles (leg curl). The average leg curl score in 1,345 middle school and high school football players was only 56% of the leg extension score. To find your ratio, divide your leg press score (in pounds) into your leg curl score. For example, if your leg press score is 85 pounds and your leg curl score 50 pounds, your ratio is 50 divided by 85, or 59%.

The hamstring muscle group is the weak link in sprinting and needs to be increased. Weight training and calisthenics can improve quadricep strength (leg press, squat, squat jumps to right angles, high knee lifts, jogging and sprinting) whereas very few exercises (leg curl) actually strengthen the hamstring muscle group. Find your leg press/leg curl ratio and record it on your test score sheet. If your leg curl score is not at least 75% of your leg extension score, check the programs "Functional strength/power training" and "Sprint loading" on your test score sheet. These programs will strengthen your hamstrings.

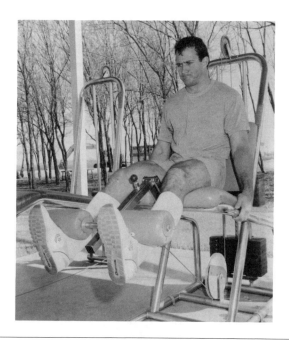

Figure 2.3a Leg extension.

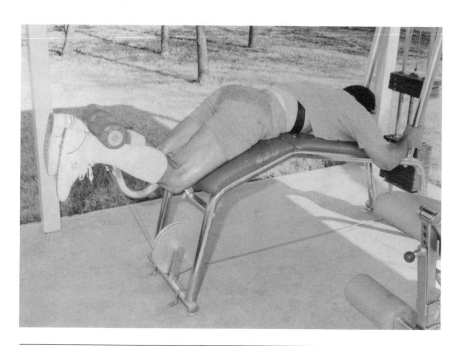

Figure 2.3b Leg curl.

Figure 2.4 Measuring stride length.

Stride Length

Place two markers 25 yards apart on a smooth dirt surface such as a baseball infield. Begin your run from a starting line about 50 yards away and be certain you are sprinting at full speed when you reach the first marker. Sprint full speed between the two markers and avoid jumping or taking an abnormally long, unnatural stride. Have your coach or friend measure the imprint of one stride from the tip of the rear toe to the tip of the front toe (Figure 2.4). Repeat the test at least twice and record the average of two strides to the nearest inch next to "Stride length" on your test score sheet.

To determine your ideal stride length (see Table 2.2), find your age group, then locate your height in inches. Then read across the table to find the range of your ideal stride length in inches. If your measured stride length is less than this range, check the programs "Plyometrics," "Sprint loading," "Sporting speed," and "Overspeed training" on your test score sheet. These programs will increase your stride length. If your stride length is greater than this range and you are sprinting without overstriding, do not change your stride.

Table 2.2 Ideal Stride Lengths by Age

Height	Stride length (in.)		
	Males 9–16	Males 17 and older	All females
50	53–61	59–67	54–62
51	54–62	61–69	55–63
52	55–63	62–70	56–64
53	56–64	63–71	57–65
54	58–66	64–72	58–66
55	59–67	66–74	59–67
56	60–68	67–75	60–68
57	61–69	68–76	62–70
58	62–70	69–77	63–71
59	63–71	71–79	64–72
60	64–72	72–80	65–73
61	66–74	73–81	66–74
62	67–75	74–82	67–75
63	68–76	76–84	68–76
64	69–77	77–85	70–78
65	70–78	78–86	71–79
66	71–79	79–87	72–80
67	72–80	81–89	73–81
68	74–82	82–90	74–82
69	75–83	83–91	75–83
70	76–84	85–93	76–84
71	77–85	86–94	78–86
72	78–86	87–95	79–87
73	79–87	88–96	80–88
74	80–88	89–97	81–89
75	82–90	91–99	82–90
76	83–91	92–100	83–91
77	84–92	93–101	85–93
78	85–93	95–103	86–94
79	86–94	96–104	87–95
80	87–95	97–105	. . .

(Cont.)

Table 2.2 (Cont.)

| Height | Stride length (in.) | | |
	Males 9–16	Males 17 and older	All females
81	88–96	98–106	. . .
82	90–98	100–108	. . .
83	91–99	101–109	. . .
84	92–100	102–110	. . .

Additional Information

You now have enough information to discover two other important things about yourself, that is, how many steps you take per second and how well you accelerate from a dead-stop, or stationary position, to full speed.

Stride Rate

To determine the number of steps you take per second while sprinting, use the stride rate matrix (Table 2.3). Find your flying 40-yard-dash time and then your stride length in inches. Read across the table to find your *stride rate*. Record this score on your test score sheet.

The stride rate of champion male sprinters approaches 5 steps per second; champion female sprinters average 4.48 steps per second. Since everyone can benefit from an improved stride rate, check "Overspeed training" on your test score sheet regardless of your score. This program will improve your stride rate.

Acceleration

Subtract your flying 40-yard time from your stationary 40-yard time and record the score to the right of "Acceleration" on your test score sheet.

Table 2.3 Stride Rate Matrix

Flying 40-yd dash

Stride length	3.6	3.7	3.8	3.9	4.0	4.1	4.2	4.3	4.4	4.5	4.6	4.7	4.8	4.9	5.0	5.1	5.2	5.3	5.4	5.5	5.6
50	8.0	7.7	7.5	7.3	7.2	7.0	6.8	6.7	6.5	6.4	6.2	6.1	6.0	5.9	5.7	5.6	5.5	5.4	5.3	5.2	5.1
51	7.8	7.6	7.4	7.2	7.0	6.8	6.7	6.5	6.4	6.2	6.1	6.0	5.8	5.7	5.6	5.5	5.4	5.3	5.2	5.1	5.0
52	7.6	7.4	7.2	7.1	6.9	6.7	6.5	6.4	6.3	6.1	6.0	5.8	5.7	5.6	5.5	5.4	5.3	5.2	5.1	5.0	4.9
53	7.5	7.3	7.1	6.9	6.7	6.6	6.4	6.3	6.1	6.0	5.9	5.7	5.6	5.5	5.4	5.3	5.2	5.1	5.0	4.9	4.8
54	7.4	7.2	7.0	6.8	6.6	6.5	6.3	6.2	6.0	5.9	5.8	5.6	5.5	5.4	5.3	5.2	5.1	5.0	4.9	4.8	4.7
55	7.2	7.0	6.9	6.7	6.6	6.4	6.2	6.0	5.9	5.8	5.7	5.6	5.4	5.3	5.2	5.1	5.0	4.9	4.8	4.7	4.6
56	7.1	6.9	6.7	6.6	6.4	6.3	6.1	6.0	5.8	5.7	5.5	5.4	5.3	5.2	5.1	5.0	4.9	4.8	4.7	4.6	4.5
57	7.0	6.8	6.7	6.5	6.3	6.1	6.0	5.9	5.8	5.7	5.5	5.4	5.3	5.2	5.1	5.0	4.9	4.8	4.7	4.6	4.5
58	6.9	6.7	6.5	6.4	6.2	6.0	5.9	5.8	5.7	5.5	5.4	5.3	5.2	5.1	5.0	4.9	4.8	4.7	4.6	4.5	4.4
59	6.8	6.6	6.4	6.3	6.1	6.0	5.8	5.7	5.6	5.4	5.3	5.2	5.1	5.0	4.9	4.8	4.7	4.6	4.5	4.4	4.3
60	6.7	6.5	6.3	6.2	6.0	5.9	5.7	5.6	5.4	5.2	5.1	5.0	4.9	4.8	4.7	4.6	4.5	4.4	4.3	4.2	4.1
61	6.6	6.4	6.2	6.1	5.9	5.7	5.6	5.5	5.4	5.3	5.1	5.0	4.9	4.8	4.7	4.6	4.5	4.4	4.3	4.2	4.1
62	6.4	6.3	6.2	6.0	5.9	5.7	5.6	5.4	5.3	5.2	5.0	4.9	4.8	4.7	4.6	4.5	4.4	4.3	4.3	4.2	4.1
63	6.3	6.1	6.0	5.8	5.7	5.6	5.5	5.3	5.2	5.1	5.0	4.9	4.8	4.7	4.6	4.5	4.4	4.3	4.2	4.1	4.0
64	6.2	6.1	5.9	5.8	5.6	5.5	5.4	5.2	5.1	5.0	4.9	4.8	4.7	4.6	4.5	4.4	4.3	4.2	4.1	4.1	4.0
65	6.2	6.0	5.8	5.7	5.6	5.4	5.3	5.2	5.0	4.9	4.8	4.7	4.6	4.5	4.4	4.3	4.2	4.1	4.0	4.0	4.0
66	6.1	5.9	5.7	5.6	5.5	5.3	5.2	5.1	5.0	4.9	4.7	4.6	4.5	4.4	4.4	4.3	4.2	4.1	4.0	4.0	3.9
67	6.0	5.8	5.7	5.6	5.4	5.3	5.1	5.0	4.9	4.8	4.7	4.6	4.5	4.4	4.3	4.2	4.1	4.0	3.9	3.9	3.8

(Cont.)

Table 2.3 (Cont.)

										Flying 40-yd dash											
Stride length	3.6	3.7	3.8	3.9	4.0	4.1	4.2	4.3	4.4	4.5	4.6	4.7	4.8	4.9	5.0	5.1	5.2	5.3	5.4	5.5	5.6
68	5.9	5.7	5.6	5.4	5.3	5.2	5.0	4.9	4.7	4.6	4.5	4.4	4.3	4.3	4.2	4.1	4.0	3.9	3.8	3.7	3.7
69	5.8	5.6	5.5	5.3	5.2	5.1	5.0	4.9	4.8	4.6	4.5	4.4	4.3	4.3	4.2	4.1	4.0	3.9	3.9	3.8	3.7
70	5.7	5.6	5.4	5.3	5.1	5.0	4.9	4.8	4.7	4.6	4.5	4.4	4.3	4.2	4.1	4.0	4.0	3.9	3.8	3.7	3.7
71	5.6	5.5	5.3	5.2	5.1	5.0	4.8	4.7	4.6	4.5	4.4	4.3	4.2	4.1	4.1	4.0	3.9	3.8	3.8	3.7	3.6
72	5.6	5.4	5.3	5.1	5.0	4.9	4.8	4.7	4.6	4.4	4.3	4.3	4.2	4.1	4.0	3.9	3.8	3.8	3.7	3.6	3.5
73	5.5	5.3	5.2	5.1	4.9	4.8	4.7	4.6	4.5	4.4	4.3	4.2	4.1	4.0	4.0	3.9	3.8	3.7	3.6	3.6	3.5
74	5.4	5.3	5.1	5.0	4.9	4.8	4.6	4.5	4.4	4.3	4.2	4.1	4.0	4.0	3.9	3.8	3.7	3.6	3.5	3.5	3.4
75	5.3	5.2	5.1	4.9	4.8	4.7	4.6	4.5	4.4	4.3	4.2	4.1	4.0	3.9	3.8	3.8	3.7	3.6	3.5	3.4	3.4
76	5.3	5.1	5.0	4.9	4.7	4.6	4.5	4.4	4.3	4.2	4.1	4.0	3.9	3.8	3.8	3.7	3.6	3.6	3.5	3.4	3.3
77	5.2	5.0	4.9	4.8	4.7	4.6	4.5	4.4	4.3	4.2	4.1	4.0	3.9	3.8	3.7	3.6	3.5	3.5	3.4	3.4	3.3
78	5.1	5.0	4.9	4.7	4.6	4.5	4.4	4.3	4.2	4.1	4.0	3.9	3.8	3.8	3.7	3.6	3.5	3.5	3.4	3.4	3.3
79	5.1	4.9	4.8	4.7	4.6	4.5	4.3	4.2	4.1	4.0	3.9	3.8	3.8	3.7	3.6	3.6	3.5	3.4	3.4	3.3	3.2
80	5.0	4.9	4.8	4.6	4.5	4.4	4.3	4.2	4.1	4.0	3.9	3.8	3.8	3.7	3.6	3.5	3.5	3.4	3.3	3.3	3.2
81	4.9	4.8	4.7	4.6	4.4	4.3	4.2	4.1	4.0	4.0	3.9	3.8	3.7	3.6	3.6	3.5	3.4	3.3	3.3	3.2	3.2
82	4.9	4.8	4.6	4.5	4.4	4.3	4.2	4.1	4.0	3.9	3.8	3.9	3.7	3.5	3.5	3.4	3.4	3.3	3.3	3.2	3.1
83	4.8	4.7	4.6	4.5	4.3	4.2	4.1	4.0	4.0	3.9	3.8	3.7	3.6	3.5	3.5	3.4	3.3	3.2	3.2	3.1	3.0
84	4.7	4.6	4.6	4.4	4.3	4.2	4.1	4.0	3.9	3.8	3.7	3.6	3.5	3.5	3.4	3.4	3.3	3.2	3.2	3.1	3.0
85	4.7	4.6	4.5	4.3	4.2	4.1	4.0	3.9	3.9	3.8	3.7	3.6	3.5	3.5	3.4	3.3	3.3	3.2	3.1	3.0	3.0
86	4.7	4.5	4.4	4.3	4.2	4.1	4.0	3.9	3.8	3.7	3.6	3.6	3.5	3.4	3.4	3.3	3.2	3.2	3.1	3.0	3.0

87	4.6	4.5	4.4	4.2	4.1	4.0	3.9	3.9	3.8	3.7	3.6	3.5	3.5	3.4	3.3	3.3	3.2	3.1	3.0	3.0	2.9
88	4.6	4.4	4.3	4.2	4.1	4.0	3.9	3.8	3.7	3.6	3.6	3.5	3.4	3.3	3.3	3.3	3.2	3.1	3.0	3.0	2.9
89	4.5	4.4	4.3	4.2	4.0	4.0	3.9	3.8	3.7	3.6	3.5	3.4	3.3	3.3	3.2	3.2	3.1	3.0	2.9	2.9	2.8
90	4.4	4.3	4.2	4.1	3.9	3.9	3.7	3.7	3.6	3.5	3.4	3.3	3.3	3.2	3.1	3.1	3.0	3.0	2.9	2.9	2.8
91	4.4	4.3	4.2	4.1	4.0	3.9	3.8	3.7	3.7	3.5	3.4	3.4	3.3	3.2	3.1	3.1	3.0	3.0	2.9	2.8	2.8
92	4.4	4.3	4.1	4.0	3.9	3.8	3.7	3.6	3.6	3.5	3.4	3.3	3.3	3.2	3.2	3.1	3.0	3.0	2.9	2.9	2.8
93	4.3	4.2	4.1	4.0	3.9	3.8	3.7	3.6	3.5	3.4	3.4	3.3	3.3	3.2	3.1	3.1	3.0	3.0	2.9	2.8	2.8
94	4.3	4.1	4.0	3.9	3.8	3.7	3.6	3.6	3.5	3.4	3.3	3.3	3.2	3.1	3.0	3.0	3.0	3.0	2.8	2.8	2.7
95	4.2	4.1	4.0	3.9	3.8	3.7	3.6	3.5	3.4	3.4	3.3	3.2	3.2	3.1	3.0	3.0	2.9	2.9	2.8	2.8	2.7
96	4.2	4.1	4.0	3.9	3.8	3.7	3.5	3.5	3.4	3.4	3.3	3.2	3.1	3.1	3.0	2.9	2.9	2.8	2.7	2.7	2.6
97	4.1	4.0	3.9	3.8	3.7	3.6	3.5	3.5	3.4	3.3	3.2	3.1	3.1	3.0	3.0	3.8	2.8	2.8	2.7	2.7	2.7
98	4.1	4.0	3.9	3.8	3.7	3.6	3.5	3.5	3.4	3.3	3.2	3.1	3.1	3.0	2.9	2.9	2.8	2.8	2.8	2.7	2.6
99	4.0	3.9	3.8	3.7	3.6	3.6	3.5	3.4	3.3	3.3	3.2	3.1	3.0	3.0	2.9	2.9	2.8	2.8	2.7	2.7	2.6
100	4.0	3.9	3.8	3.7	3.6	3.5	3.4	3.4	3.3	3.3	3.2	3.1	3.0	3.0	2.9	2.9	2.8	2.7	2.7	2.6	2.6
101	4.0	3.9	3.8	3.7	3.6	3.5	3.4	3.4	3.3	3.3	3.2	3.1	3.0	3.0	2.9	2.9	2.8	2.7	2.7	2.6	2.6
102	3.9	3.8	3.7	3.6	3.5	3.4	3.3	3.3	3.2	3.1	3.1	3.0	3.0	3.0	2.9	2.8	2.8	2.7	2.7	2.6	2.5
103	3.9	3.8	3.7	3.6	3.5	3.4	3.3	3.3	3.2	3.1	3.1	3.0	3.0	2.9	2.9	2.8	2.8	2.7	2.6	2.6	2.5
104	3.9	3.7	3.6	3.6	3.5	3.4	3.3	3.3	3.2	3.1	3.1	3.0	3.0	2.9	2.9	2.8	2.7	2.7	2.6	2.5	2.4
105	3.8	3.7	3.6	3.5	3.4	3.3	3.2	3.2	3.1	3.1	3.1	2.9	2.9	2.8	2.8	2.7	2.7	2.6	2.6	2.5	2.4
106	3.8	3.6	3.6	3.5	3.4	3.3	3.2	3.2	3.1	3.1	3.0	2.9	2.9	2.8	2.7	2.7	2.7	2.6	2.5	2.5	2.4
107	3.7	3.6	3.5	3.4	3.3	3.2	3.1	3.1	3.0	3.0	2.9	2.8	2.8	2.7	2.7	2.6	2.6	2.5	2.5	2.5	2.4
108	3.7	3.6	3.5	3.4	3.3	3.2	3.1	3.1	3.0	3.0	2.9	2.8	2.8	2.7	2.6	2.6	2.5	2.5	2.4	2.4	2.3

Prepared by Lynne R. Mohn

The difference in time between your stationary 40-yard dash and your flying 40-yard dash is due to *acceleration*. If there is more than a .7-second difference between these two scores, check the program "Ballistics," "Plyometrics," "Sprint loading," and "Sporting speed" (starting form) on your test score sheet. These training programs will improve your acceleration time. A quick way to find out how fast you now should be sprinting a 40-yard dash is to add .7 seconds to your flying 40-yard-dash time. For example, if your stationary 40 is 4.9 seconds and your flying 40 is 4.0 seconds, you should be sprinting the stationary 40 in 4.7 seconds (flying 40 of 4.0 + .7 seconds = 4.7), not in 4.9 seconds. The .2 seconds difference is probably due to faulty starting techniques. Chapter 3 gives you numerous tips to correct these problems.

The National Association of Speed and Explosion (NASE) has developed a test to predict speed potential. It estimates how much you should be able to improve. This is your fifth and final test.

NASE Future 40-Yard Dash

Have your coach or friend test you in the 40-yard dash from a stationary start using surgical tubing to tow you as fast as possible. Connect your belt securely around your waist with the other belt attached to a partner. While your partner stands at the finish line, back up and stretch the tubing exactly 40 yards until you reach the starting line. Then assume a three-point or track stance. The timer stands at the finish line, starts a stopwatch on your first muscular movement, and stops it when you cross the finish line. After you sprint only 5 yards, your partner sprints as fast as possible away from you to give you additional pull throughout the test. Record your score to the right of the "NASE future 40 test" on your test score sheet.

Your time in this test, plus .3 seconds, gives an estimate of what you are capable of doing after several months of training using the 7-Step Model for speed improvement.

How to Use Your Test Scores

You now have enough information to design a speed improvement program just for you. (A more comprehensive testing program is described in Appendix B.) For each test, check (✔) "Yes" in the "Weakness?" column on your test score sheet if you failed to meet the specified standard. Check the appropriate training program(s) listed in the far right column. You will need to follow these programs to eliminate your weaknesses. Each of these programs and the 7-Step Model for speed improvement are described in detail in chapter 3. Sample workouts are also shown to help you organize your training schedule.

Study the example below to see exactly how the plan works.

Al Steihl, age 17, is a 6-ft, 190-lb halfback on the football team. His test scores were as follows:

Test	Score	Comments
Stationary 40	4.9 sec	Good; can be improved
Flying 40	4.0 sec	Good; can be improved
Acceleration time (flying 40 − stationary 40)	.9 sec	Poor; suggests faulty starting form or lack of explosive power; exceeds minimum standard of .7 sec; can be improved through ballistics training (Step 3), sprint loading (Step 5), and sporting speed training (Step 6)

Speed endurance:
  Time from 40- to 80-yd mark
  Time from 80- to 120-yd mark
	4.0 sec
	4.4 sec
		Poor; difference of .4 sec between two 40-yd areas suggests poor speed endurance; athlete is slowing down too much due to fatigue; can be improved through sprint loading (Step 5) and speed endurance training (Step 6)

NASE future 40 test	4.2 sec	Your potential best 40-yd time is 4.5 sec (4.2 + .3 = 4.5).
Leg strength (leg press score)	400 lb	Poor; less than 2.5 times body weight of 190 lb; minimum score should be 475 lb.

Leg strength (hamstring/ quadricep strength:		
Leg extension (quadricep)	180 lb	Poor; hamstring strength is only 50% of quadricep strength (90 ÷ 180 = 50%); leg curl should be improved to 135 lb (75% of quadricep strength); can be improved through basic training (Step 1), functional strength/power training (Step 2), and sprint loading (Step 5).
Leg curl (hamstring)	90 lb	
Stride length	80 in.	Poor; Al appears to be understriding. As shown in Table 2.2, a 19-year-old who is 72 in. tall should take an 87–95-in. stride; can be improved through plyometric training (Step 4), sporting speed training (Step 6), and overspeed training (Step 7)
Stride rate	4.5 steps	Good; according to Table 2.3, a stride length of 80 in. and a flying 40-yd time of 4.0 sec results in an estimated 4.5 steps per second; can be improved through overspeed training (Step 7)

Concentrating on the Correct Areas for Your Sport

No matter what your sport is, there are only five ways to improve your speed in short distances:

- Improve your reaction time and starting ability.
- Improve your acceleration time (reach full speed faster).
- Increase the length of your stride.
- Increase the number of steps you take per second (stride rate).
- Improve your speed endurance.

These areas are not equally important to athletes in all sports. For example, defensive backs and linebackers in football are generally moving at one-fourth to one-half speed when they go into a full-speed sprint rather than starting from a stationary position like a baseball player. For these athletes, starting technique is not nearly as important as are acceleration, stride rate, stride length, and speed endurance. For track and baseball athletes, starting technique from the blocks, the batting box, and positions in the field is important.

Although improving your speed endurance (anaerobic conditioning) will not make you faster, it will keep you from slowing down due to fatigue after repeated short sprints or at the end of a long sprint of 80 yards or more. This quality is important to most team-sport athletes.

Study Table 2.4 carefully. The key speed improvement areas for each sport are listed in order of importance and help you use your test scores to focus on the appropriate programs for your specific sport. If, for example, your test scores indicate that you need to improve your starting technique and you are a defensive back on the football team, you can ignore that finding and concentrate on more important areas that are critical to your position.

Keep in mind that speed improvement requires a holistic approach. In other words, each part of the 7-Step Model discussed in chapter 3 is very important. Although you will train in each area, your test results and the key speed improvement areas for your sport indicate the areas that require your attention.

You are now ready to begin your speed improvement program.

Table 2.4 Speed Improvement Attack Areas for Football, Basketball, and Baseball

Sport	Attack areas (by priority)	Comment
Football	1. Acceleration 2. Stride rate 3. Stride length 4. Speed endurance 5. Starting ability	You sprint faster in the open field only by taking faster or longer steps. Speed endurance is important only to prevent you from slowing down after repeated short sprints.
Basketball	1. Acceleration 2. Stride rate 3. Speed endurance	Most explosive action occurs after some slight movement has taken place (e.g., a jog, a bounce, a sideward movement). Maxi-

(Cont.)

Table 2.4 (Cont.

Sport	Attack areas (by priority)	Comment
	4. Starting ability 5. Stride length	mum speed is never attained. Acceleration, stride rate, and speed endurance should receive the most emphasis.
Baseball	1. Starting ability 2. Acceleration 3. Stride rate 4. Stride length	A baseball player will not approach maximum speed unless he hits a triple or an inside-the-park home run. Starting ability and acceleration should receive the most emphasis.

Chapter 3

Steps to Speed Improvement

If you should put even a little on a little, and should do this often, soon this too would become big.
—Hesiod

In chapter 2, you learned the answers to the first two of the four questions about sprinting faster:

- How fast do I need to be?
- How fast am I today?
- How do I train to get faster?
- How do I apply my newly found speed to my sport?

Now let us move on to the 7-Step Model and answer the third and fourth questions.

The 7-Step Model

The 7-Step Model contains the secrets used by the privileged few great speedsters of the past who built their speed of the future today. Each of the 7 steps brings you closer to achieving tomorrow's speed. This model is a commonsense approach that, first, recognizes how your body works and, second, builds a series of practical steps that systematically guide you to new unimaginable speeds. Try to feel the moment of success as you break away from the competition. Each of these steps is crucial in training for the physical demands that your newly found speed will be placing on your body. Drink in the strength and wisdom that each step provides you, and climb the staircase to your athletic dreams!

Our bodies contain all the wisdom of the ages. One generation continues to pass on the essentials for survival to the next. This ancient wisdom tells us to be ready for the future. In the case of sport speed, you should develop all the tools that are needed to sprint faster as early in your career as possible. What are these tools? They are simply the basic systems of the body that serve us in the following ways:

- *Communication and control*. You must "train" your brain or nervous system to be fast. Give the nervous system the opportunity to experience actions that will assist it in making split-second decisions. Slow-thinking programs must be replaced by faster motor programs.
- *Biomechanics (the neuromuscular and leverage systems)*. The nervous system plus the bones, joints, and muscular system must be properly trained.
- *Cardioaerobics*. A high level of cardiovascular/respiratory fitness is essential to high-level performance.
- *High-speed fuel system*. The fuel supply provides the energy for acceleration, power, and speed in football, basketball, and baseball.
- *Supernutrition*. You must acquire the knowledge of sound nutrition, high energy intake, energy expenditure, fluid replacement, growth and repair of body tissue, and a sound method of gaining body weight and muscle bulk (see chapter 5).

The 7-Step Model categorizes various forms of exercise into 7 conceptual steps. Each step takes the athlete to another level of speed that requires a faster rate of operation (force must be applied at an ever-increasing rate). This model begins with basic training at Step 1, where total body tissue and systems efficiency are developed to sustain the impacts of higher overspeed training in the 7th step, where speeds exceed the normal sporting and sprinting speed by 10%–20%. To improve speed in short distances, a holistic approach is required; in other words, all 7 steps are important. After you have acquired a solid foundation at Steps 1 and 2, you will progress into high- and super-high-speed training where you will focus on the specific act of sprinting and sprinting-type movements by using specialized techniques. Nutrition is the foundation of the 7-Step Model. Without proper sports nutrition, the very best speed improvement training program will yield limited results, and training gains and performance will be negated.

Step 1: Basic training

Pure strength/muscle endurance. Develops all qualities of human movement to a level that will provide a solid base to build each successive step. Basic training includes programs to increase body control and sustained effort (muscular and cardiovascular/anaerobic and aerobic).

Step 2: Functional strength/power

Explosive movements against medium to heavy resistance. Maximum power is trained by working in an intensity range of 55%–85% maximum.

Step 3: Ballistics

High-speed sending and receiving movements.

Step 4: Plyometrics

Explosive hopping, jumping, bounding, hitting and kicking.

Step 5: Sprint loading

Precision loading at high speed. Intensity of 85%–100% of maximum speed.

Step 6: Sporting speed/speed endurance

Actual participation in the sport and/or skills involved in the sport.

Step 7: Overspeed training

Systematic application of sporting speed that exceeds maximum speed by 10%–20% through the use of various training techniques.

Step 1: Basic Training: Develop a Solid Foundation

Basic training serves an "all systems go" function. Exercises performed in Step 1 of the 7-Step Model provide a solid foundation to help accelerate you to the top floor—the 7th step. Basic training includes walking, running, jumping, dancing, martial arts of all types, and games and sports.

Experts have called Step 1 a period of general preparation because its major objective is to mobilize all the body's resources before you begin to work on increasing your speed. Basic training also includes other organizational elements that are necessary in the operation of the total program. The programs suggested for each element are examples of the many different ways of achieving the objectives of Step 1.

Basic Training Sports Check

Before you venture too far into your planning, we recommend that you take a close look at your *basic training fitness*. This is important because you will be building your high-speed training on this foundation. Here is how it fits into a basic sports check. There are five elements in the sports check, and these are listed below in order of importance. Each element is vital to your success in sprinting faster. You will find that you already are involved in many of the key aspects of basic training—Step 1 of the 7-Step Model.

Sports-Specific Tasks

Sports-specific tasks should be determined with the help of a professionally qualified person. Each of the tasks that make up your sport must be evaluated and grouped according to (a) how frequent the task is, (b) how difficult the task is, and (c) how critical the task is. Remember that your training, to be effective, must match these job requirements. Deficiencies in performance must also be given additional attention. There can be no substitute for this first step.

Training the brain by using every means possible to make it an even faster processor of information has been overlooked until recently. It is now becoming common knowledge that you can gain more control over the nervous system than you ever dreamed possible. What was once considered trickery is now being shown in reputable research to be trainable human functions. To accelerate your speed to uncommon levels is a job for the space-age technology that is emerging from these laboratories today. You must recognize that speed in running or in games must be developed and switched on and off precisely for you to be able to sprint and play fast. A few of the more important findings from these studies that will help you sprint faster are listed below.

High-Speed Action

Sprinting or game action takes place at such high speeds that thinking interferes with performance. Players must react to the situation and ask questions later.

Brain Research. Brain research favors the use of the ''flow state'' (alpha 8–13 hertz brainwave) for producing high levels of game performance. Flow state reduces dwelling on errors, which invariably produces more errors.

Visual Awareness. Visual awareness can be controlled so that everything in the visual field can be seen. The running back who sees all defensive players as they are positioned and then runs to ''daylight'' is using a technique called *open focus*, a term coined by Les Fehmi. It is the ultimate camera that takes a clear picture (without a shutter) of anything it wants at any time, even at the same time that another picture is taken. This *is* possible. If you can process all the information you need in your sport, your performance in every phase of that sport will be greatly improved.

Adaptation to High Speed. Many of us have experienced the adaptation to high-speed travel. Driving at 80 miles per hour initially seems fast due to acceleration and the relative speeds and positions of other cars or objects in the field of vision. However, in a short period of time, this sensation is replaced by a sense that 80 miles per hour is not fast at all. This is the sensation we want you to develop on the playing field. Our programs for speed of movement and thought provide exercises that improve this flow-state condition. At a recent dance concert, an Irish step dancer demonstrated unimaginable artistry of footwork. The speed and precision of his complicated foot patterns were beyond description. Sixteen years of arduous practice came alive through the fleeting flurry of shoes and feet. As I sat there spellbound, my mind raced almost as fast as his feet in an attempt to match what I was seeing with how it could be used for training athletes to sprint faster. The conclusion was very simple: Include dance as part of the training program.

Dance and Sport. Dance in physical education programs is nothing new. Many school curricula in the United States offer dance classes. However, this fact does not insure that usable principles and skills are always transferred to athletics. Therefore, we suggest that you select dance classes from instructors who understand the relationships between cognitive and motor programming and who apply neuromuscular and rhythm training essential for your sport.

Training Your Recessive (Nondominant) Side.   Training both sides of the body by developing near-equal skill in both hands and feet appears to improve skill levels by producing higher levels of synchrony or coordination in the nervous system. Research has shown that sprinters and cyclists produce uneven amounts of power output with the legs. This is an example of dominant and recessive motor patterns that can limit speed of movement. Training can produce a more even power output in the recessive leg (generally the weaker of the two) and thereby increase the total power and speed of the runner.

Motorvator Game.   Twenty-first-century computers have helped create a game—the Motorvator—that helps to train the brain and the total neuromuscular system (Figure 3.1). Alternate hand and foot patterns, along with running patterns (i.e., left arm, right leg),

Figure 3.1 Motorvator game.

have been programmed into the game. These specific patterns and their rhythms are used systematically to guide the player to higher levels of hand and footwork. A powerful advantage of using the Motorvator is its ability to record correct responses. There is evidence that specific benefits such as structural and functional changes in the nervous system can be gained by playing this game, which may help you sprint faster.

Body Control

The major quality that we want to train under body control is the ability to learn to move in a variety of ways quickly. A general program should include quickness and agility along with the ability to use all parts of the body. These abilities must include striking with the hands and feet. All sorts of gymnastics and games are essential. Basketball, handball, martial arts, and dance are a few of the best activities for gaining good body control.

Power

Many people mistakenly believe that power and strength are the same. The difference, however, can be shown by the example of the straw and the oak tree. If you take a straw and push it against the oak tree with your hand, what happens? The straw crumples quite easily. Perhaps you think that if the strength of the straw is increased 2, 4, 6, or even 10 times, the straw will then penetrate the oak tree. This is not true. Although increasing the strength of the straw is important, it would still crumple quickly on contacting the tree. The most efficient way for the straw to go through the oak is to increase its speed. With the proper combination of the straw's weight, acceleration, and speed, it can penetrate the mighty oak. You have seen Walter Payton run over defensive players nearly twice his size. He does this with the same combination of weight, acceleration, and speed.

This principle can also be experienced in baseball. Imagine the feeling you had when playing catch or fielding a ball traveling at various speeds with and without a glove. The faster the ball was thrown, the more pain and difficulty there was catching it bare-handed, in spite of the fact that a baseball is a rather light object. Even with a light baseball, speed greatly increases the force and impact when it strikes your glove.

Strength

In chapter 2, leg strength tests were given to determine the strength levels of these important muscles used in sprinting. Acceptable levels of strength are also essential for the total body. We recommend the following additional tests and standards for developing general strength and explosive power: jerk—1.3 times body weight (p. 37), clean—1.3 times body weight (p. 37), dead lift—1.9 times body weight (p. 42), squat—1.9 times body weight (p. 42), and bench press—1.4 times body weight (p. 46).

Cardioaerobics

An important training principle requires developing acceptable levels of fitness prior to working in your sport of interest. The circulatory and respiratory systems must be brought to levels that can easily handle the specific demands of your sport. Many aerobic exercises have been proposed for training and evaluating aerobic fitness. You should strive to meet the standards listed, never falling below the category "Good" even when you are untrained and striving for the category "Excellent" or "Superior" when you are highly trained for your sport.

1.5-Mile Test in Minutes and Seconds		
Men	10:16–12:00	Good
Women	11:16–13:00	
Men	8:45–10:15	Excellent
Women	9:46–10:45	
Men	Under 8:45	Superior
Women	Under 9:45	

Basic training serves as a sneak preview of things to come. It is a brief introduction that prepares you for the rigors that lay ahead. Certain goals should be established as a result of your sports check evaluation. Simple tests are provided in chapter 2. Each goal will serve as a guide for improving your basic fitness before advancing to your next step. The next section will lead you through the necessary steps for developing a basic training program. It also allows you the flexibility of writing more advanced programs in the future.

Organizing Your Program

Complete the sports check evaluation sheet (Table 3.1). Develop a list of the areas you need to work on and list those areas in order of importance relative to your main objective. Next, complete the conditioning program schedule (Table 3.2). Place your list on this sheet in the space provided. Record each exercise in the day and time period of your choice. This will be your workout schedule of exercises that will remove any of your measured weaknesses.

It is important that you commit yourself to the program by writing your name on the signature line.

Elements of Your Basic Training Program

Now let us take a closer look at the basic training program and the elements that are included. Every good workout should have a primary purpose. A workout is similar to any work of art, whether it be a book, dance, or play in that there is a beginning, a main body, and an ending. The beginning prepares the way for the main

Table 3.1 Sports Check Evaluation Sheet

Test area	Weakness		Program	
Sports-specific tasks	___ Yes ___ No		List actual skills and develop a program for their improvement	
Training the brain	___ Yes ___ No	☐ Juggling ☐ Dance	☐ Martial arts ☐ Games (physical and mental)	
Body control	___ Yes ___ No	☐ Motorvator ☐ Basketball ☐ Handball ☐ Dance	☐ Gymnastics ☐ Handball/ racquetball ☐ Martial arts	
Power/strength	___ Yes ___ No	☐ Power ☐ Strength endurance	☐ Maximum strength	
Cardioaerobics	___ Yes ___ No	☐ 1.5-mi run ☐ Other	☐ 880-yd run	

Note. If a weakness is found, check the training programs to the right that are designed to correct the weakness.

Table 3.2 Conditioning Program Schedule

Name _____   Ht _____   Wt _____   Date/Time _____

Time	Mon.	Tue.	Wed.	Thurs.	Fri.	Sat.	Sun.
9:00 A.M. to 11:00 A.M.							
11:00 A.M. to 1:00 P.M.							
1:00 P.M. to 3:00 P.M.							
3:00 P.M. to 5:00 P.M.							
5:00 P.M. to 7:00 P.M.							

purpose, and the ending gets you back to a normal level of operation. This theme is evident in any step of the 7-Step Model.

Warm-Up

Warm-up sessions increase your body temperature, circulation, and muscle elasticity and prepare you psychologically for the routine ahead. Choose your routine from the list below. Remember, you should stretch only after elevating your heart rate.

Jog 440–880 Yards in 5 Minutes.   This should be easy-paced, enjoyable running with a progressive increase in pace as you approach the final 200 yards.

Jump Rope for 3–6 Minutes.   The time can be broken into rounds that emphasize various foot and hand rhythms.

Use a Speed Bag or Shadow Box for 3–6 Minutes.   The time can be divided into rounds that emphasize various foot and hand combinations and rhythms.

Juggle for 3–6 Minutes.   A variety of juggling techniques should be used. Two or three bags of various textures and weights can be used along with more advanced techniques such as a mini-trampoline or bong board. These methods fit nicely into a warm-up routine and provide an integrated way of training the brain and the neuromuscular system.

Flexibility (Stretching) Exercises for 10–15 Minutes.   The following static flexibility exercises are excellent choices to improve your total body-joint range of motion and prepare you for sprint training:

- *Hamstring group (back of upper leg).* Exercise 1: Stand erect with both knees bent slightly. Bend over and touch the ground, holding your maximum stretch position.
  Exercise 2: Lie on your back, sit up, and reach for your toes with both knees slightly bent, holding your maximum stretch position. Keep both knees slightly bent in both exercises to remove pressure from your lower back.
- *Quadricep group (front of upper leg).* Stand on your left leg, grasp your right ankle with your right hand, and pull your heel toward your buttocks, holding your maximum stretch position. Repeat using your other leg.
- *Hip.* Lie on your back, relax, and straighten both legs. Pull the left foot toward your chest and hold. Repeat using the right foot.
- *Groin.* Assume a sitting position with the soles of your feet together. Place your hands around your feet and pull yourself forward.
- *Calf.* Stand about 2 feet from a wall and lean forward with the lead leg bent and the rear leg extended. Move the hips forward and keep the heel of the straight leg on the ground until you feel a stretch in your calf.
- *Achilles tendon and soleus.* Stand approximately 2 feet from a wall or fence. Bend the back knee slightly, keep both heels on the ground, and lean forward.

Hold the stretched positions at your maximum range of motion for 25–30 seconds and perform at least 3 sets of each exercise. Approach this session with an attitude of relaxation. You should begin the stretching session after your heart rate and body temperature have been elevated by a general warm-up such as a slow jog.

Balance for 30–60 Seconds.   Stand on one foot for 30 seconds. Increase the difficulty by moving the leg in circles or in figure eights. Repeat using your other leg.

Step 2: Weight Training: Improve Your Functional Strength and Power

The ability to generate high levels of power output is essential to peak performance and provides you with a definite advantage. Remember that power output refers simply to how fast you can do work. The relationship of work and power can be illustrated by doing a simple task—move a hundred 10-pound weights onto a 1-foot-high speed train in 10 seconds. The train will depart in 10 seconds, so only the weights on the train can be credited to your account. It is important to understand that you must train for the specific power output demands required in various sports. Table 3.3 summarizes the power output for an athlete who moves 10 weights in a 10-second period. The key point to remember is that there are only .1–.3 seconds to apply additional force. Therefore, the only way to increase your speed of action is to accelerate (increase the speed of work) the speed at which the 10-pound weights are moved.

Table 3.3 Power Output

Total pounds available	Total pounds possible in 10 secs	Total work in 10 secs	Total power in 10 secs
1,000	$10 \times 10 = 100$ lb	100 lb $\times 1$ ft $=$ 100 ft lb	$\dfrac{100 \text{ ft lb}}{10 \text{ sec}} = 10$ ft lb/sec
100%	10%	10%	10%

The results of your efforts show that you were credited with only 10% of the power and work that was possible. Only the work and power you recorded in the allotted time counted. Training to sprint fast is very similar to this example. In sprinting, the foot is in contact with the ground for about .1 seconds. Any power that is not applied at the foot during this .1-second period is of no use in running faster. Since the ''work fast to be fast'' principle is essential in all explosive sports, we recommend using high-power-output exercises with weights to train the body both mentally and physically.

Many exercises, as well as their variations, can be used to develop power output; however, the most commonly used group is traditionally called the Olympic-type lifts. These exercises provide an excellent means of training for power. Since Olympic lifts usually do not involve a trunk-twisting action when performed with a barbell, a one-hand dumbbell variation is highly recommended as a way to complement the barbell exercises.

The Olympic Lifts

Power exercises, such as the Olympic lifts, should be included in your program because (a) the body is trained to develop peak force; (b) the amount of time that peak force is applied is increased; and (c) more force is developed in a short period of time.

Clean (Barbell/Dumbbell)

The major purpose of the clean is to develop the large muscles of the body in an explosive action that requires the use of many joints and muscle groups in a coordinated movement (Figure 3.2). The following suggestions will help you perform the clean correctly:

1. Assume a comfortable stance with your feet spread about shoulder width apart.
2. Grasp the bar at slightly wider than shoulder width. An overhand, hooked strap can be used.
3. Bend your legs at the start of the lift and use the legs first.
4. Keep your back straight and hold it tightly in that position.
5. Place your shoulders under the bar.
6. Keep the bar close to your body.
7. Rebend the legs after clearing the knees.
8. Keep your arms straight, keeping in mind that this is a leg and back exercise.

Figure 3.2   Bill Bates demonstrates the clean.

9. Jump vertically into the lift with your legs, pulling the bar as high as possible. Your arms will blend in after the leg and back action.
10. Drive your elbows up.
11. Drop quickly and catch the bar on your shoulders while bringing the elbows under the bar.

Near-maximum weight will require that you go into a deep knee bend to catch the bar; therefore, strong legs are essential in good lifting.

Jerk (Barbell, Barbell from Rack, Dumbbell, and Machine)

The major purpose of the jerk is to develop the large muscle groups of the body with an action that is multijointed. This is done explosively (Figure 3.3). The following suggestions will help you perform the jerk correctly:

1. Take the bar from the rack to work primarily on the jerking movement.
2. Assume a comfortable stance with your feet spread about shoulder width apart.

Figure 3.3 Jerk.

3. Grasp the bar slightly wider than shoulder width.
4. Rest the bar primarily on your shoulders.
5. Keep your back vertical and tight.
6. Bend your legs with a quick dipping action. Experience will help you find the proper depth for a quick, explosive return.
7. Jump explosively into the bar, attempting to throw the bar as high as possible. The bar should move vertically overhead. The action of your shoulders and arms will blend into the explosive action of the jump.
8. Drop directly beneath the bar, catching it straight over the shoulders. The legs can be kept shoulder width or split.
9. Experiment to determine which foot to place forward.
10. Straighten your arms vertically, holding them (along with the rest of the body) very rigid.
11. Return to the erect position by moving the front foot back first with a slight jab step (this shortens the distance) and then step forward with your back foot.

Snatch (Barbell and Dumbbell)

The major purpose of the snatch is to develop explosiveness of the muscle groups of the body in a coordinated multijointed action

Figure 3.4   Snatch, final movement.

(Figure 3.4). The following suggestions will help you perform the snatch correctly:

1. Assume a comfortable stance with your feet spread about shoulder width apart.
2. Widen the clean grip so that the height of the bar will be lower and, therefore, will require less vertical work. Experience will help to determine the choice of grip.
3. Bend your legs before lifting the bar and use them first in the lift.
4. Keep your back straight and hold it tightly.
5. Place your shoulders over the bar.
6. Keep the bar close to your body.
7. Rebend your legs after clearing the knees.
8. Keep your arms straight to allow the legs and back to lift the bar as high as possible.
9. Jump vertically into the lift with the legs, pulling the bar with the arms as high as possible. The arms will fit into the action after the legs and back have done their part.
10. Drive your elbows up.
11. Drop quickly and catch the bar directly over your head and shoulders.

Remember that leg strength is essential in all aspects of lifting, but it is especially important in the recovery phase when lifting maximum weight.

Sample Power Output Program

The "Speed Week" principle (see chapter 4) requires high-intensity work to be done Monday through Wednesday. Therefore, a power exercise program using Olympic lifts would be included on Monday and Wednesday, after you have done your overspeed and sporting speed programs. A sample program is shown below:

Monday	Wednesday
Warm-up	**Warm-up**
Cleans:	*Jerks:*
3–6 sets	3–6 sets
3–5 repetitions	3–5 repetitions
65%–100% intensity (RM)	65%–100% intensity (RM)
Jerks:	*Cleans:*
3–6 sets	3–6 sets
3–5 repetitions	3–5 repetitions
65%–100% intensity (RM)	65%–100% intensity
1.5–5 min rest between sets	1.5–5 min rest between sets

The power component in this step will be useful as you progress to Step 3, Ballistics, where time for work output decreases at a tremendous rate and loads on the body increase.

Functional Strength Program for the Serious Athlete

The components of the complete workout schedule remain the same during the preseason period; however, their intensity and duration increase during the second half of this period. In the first half of the preseason, you should begin most of the exercises at about 50% of your maximum level. The rate of increase should be 8%–10% per week if previous maximum levels are to be regained by the time you begin your exercises for the second half of the preseason, which will involve many sets and repetitions at a high percentage of your maximum for each lift.

Another objective of the preseason's second half is to increase muscle endurance by increasing the intensity of your workout, which requires a comparable increase in the number of sets (at least 5 sets in most areas); as a consequence, the length of the standard (ideal) workout will increase from 2 to 3 hours.

A standard program is outlined below to help you get started:

1. **Warm-up, flexibility, body control, and running or jumping techniques**
   a. Jog half a mile and/or jump rope (5 min)
   b. Speed bag (15 min)
   c Flexibility: Running or jumping (10 min)

2. **Power position exercises (40 min)**
   a. Snatch—power
   b. Snatch—split-squat
   c. Clean and push jerk
   d. Pull

3. **Legs and back (23 min)**
   a. Dead lift
   b. Squats, front
   c. Squats, back
      (3–5 sets, 3–5 repetitions)

4. **Shoulders and arms (18 min)**
   a. Incline
   b. Bench
   c. Curls
      (3–5 sets, 3–5 repetitions)

5. **Abdominal and neck (9 min)**
   a. Sit-ups—3 sets, 25 repetitions
   b. Partner 4-way neck—1 set, 8–12 repetitions
   c. Rotary neck—1 set, 6 repetitions each way

Table 3.4 and Figure 3.5 a–f show a sample program for the beginner. Three sets of the leg press exercise would be performed, the first at 60% of your maximum for 10 repetitions, the second set at 65% of your maximum for 8 repetitions, and the third set at 70% of your maximum for 6 repetitions. The same procedure should be followed for each exercise.

Table 3.4 Sample Functional Strength Program (Beginner)

Exercise	RM	Mon.	Tues.	Wed.	Thurs.	Fri.	Sat. Sun.
Warm-up: Flexibility			Before every workout				
Leg/back:							
Leg press		L		M		H	
Knee extensions		L		M		H	
Knee flexion		L		M		H	
Toe raises		L		M		H	
Shoulders/arms:							
Lat pull-down		M		H		L	
Bench press		M		H		L	
Press (seated)		H		M		L	
Press (standing)		H		M		L	
Curls (dumbbells)		M		H		L	
Trunk/abdomen:							
Sit-up (bent knee)		3 × 15		3 × 15		3 × 15	
Neck:							
Partner 4-way neck		3 × 8–12		3 × 8–12		3 × 8–12	

% Repetition Maximum – Sets – Repetitions		
Light (L)	Medium (M)	Heavy (H)
60% 1 × 10	60% 1 × 10	60% 1 × 10
65% 1 × 8	70% 1 × 8	75% 1 × 8
70% 1 × 6	80% 1 × 6	70% 1 × 6

Figure 3.5a Dead lift.

Figure 3.5b Front squat.

Figure 3.5c Back squat.

Figure 3.5d Leg press.

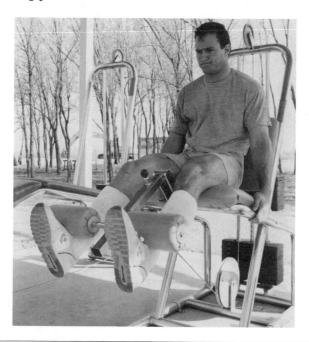

Figure 3.5e Knee extension.

Figure 3.5f Toe raises.

A sample program for the athlete at the intermediate stage of strength development is shown in Table 3.5 and Figure 3.6 a–f. A workout would involve 3 sets of each exercise with the first set at 60% of your maximum for 5–8 repetitions, the second set at 65% of your maximum for 5–8 repetitions, and the third set at 70% of your maximum for 5–8 repetitions.

The advanced program shown in Table 3.6 is programmed for high intensity. Four sets are performed with the first set at 60% of your maximum for 5 repetitions, the second set at 75% of your maximum for 3 repetitions, the third set at 85% of your maximum for 3 repetitions, and the fourth set at 90% of your maximum for 2 repetitions.

Table 3.5 Sample Functional Strength Program (Intermediate)

Exercise	RM	Mon.	Tues.	Wed.	Thurs.	Fri.	Sat.	Sun.
Warm-Up: Flexibility				Before every workout				
Power: Clean		H		M		L		
Legs and back:								
Squat		L		M		H		
Dead lift: Leg		M		H		L		
Knee extensions		M		H		L		
Shoulders:								
Bench press		H		M		L		
Press (seated, behind neck)		M		H		L		
Rowing (bent over)		L		M		H		
Trunk/abdomen:								
Sit-ups (medicine ball)		2 × 12		2 × 12		2 × 12		
Sit-ups (crunch)		3 × 25		3 × 25		3 × 25		
Trunk (hyperextension)		2 × 12		2 × 12		2 × 12		
Neck:								
Partner 4-way neck		3 × 8–12		3 × 8–12		3 × 8–12		

% Repetition Maximum – Sets – Repetitions

Light (L)	Medium (M)	Heavy (H)
60% 1 × 5–8	50% 1 × 5–8	60% 1 × 5–8
65% 1 × 5–8	70% 1 × 5–8	75% 1 × 5
70% 1 × 5–8	80% 1 × 5	85% 1 × 5

Figure 3.6a Bench press.

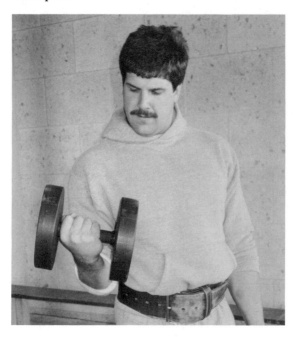

Figure 3.6b Curls.

Figure 3.6c Lat pulldown.

Figure 3.6d Flys, supine.

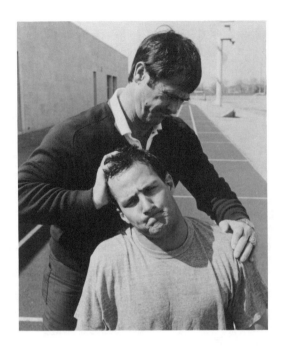

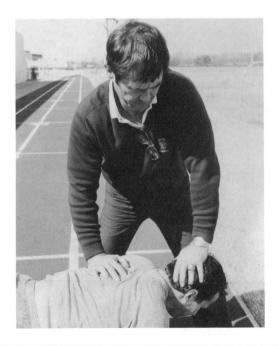

Figure 3.6e Four-way neck.

Table 3.6 Sample Functional Strength Program (Advanced)

Exercise	RM	Mon.	Tues.	Wed.	Thurs.	Fri.	Sat. Sun.
Warm-up: Flexibility				Before every workout			
Power:							
Clean, power		M		H			
Snatch, power			M		H		
Jerk, rack		H		M		L	
Legs/back:							
Pull, clean		M		L		H	
Dead lift, s/l		H		M			
Squat		L		M		H	
Squat, front						M	
Shoulders/chest/arms:							
Bench press		H		M			
Incline press			M		H		
Rowing		H		M		L	
Flys, supine				L		M	
Trunk/abdomen:							
Trunk hyperextension				3 × 10 (60%)		3 × 10 (70%)	
Sit-ups (bent knee)		3 × 25		3 × 25 (60%)		3 × 25 (70%)	
Neck:							
Partner 4-way neck		3 × 8-12		3 × 8-12		3 × 8-12	

% Repetitions Maximum – Sets – Repetitions

Light (L)	Medium (M)	Heavy (H)
60% 1 × 5	60% 1 × 5	60% 1 × 5
65% 1 × 5	70% 1 × 5	75% 1 × 3
70% 1 × 5	80% 1 × 5	85% 1 × 3
		90% 1 × 2

Table 3.7 lists performance standards for various functional strength exercises to help you set your target goals.

Strengthening the Hamstring Muscle Groups: A Unique Approach

We mentioned previously that the hamstring muscle group (back of the upper leg) could be a sprinter's weakest link. The leg curl and leg extension tests described in chapter 2 estimate the comparative strength of the quadricep (front of the upper leg) and hamstring muscle groups. Only a few elite athletes—such as some champion sprinters, power lifters like world champion Dr. Fred "Squat" Hatfield, and some defensive backs in football (backward sprinting develops the hamstring group)—are equally strong in both muscle groups. In over 15 years of speed clinics and camps, only one athlete had equal strength in both muscle groups; most failed to meet our minimum standard (hamstring strength should equal 75% of quadricep strength).

The power exercises described previously are excellent hamstring exercises as is the leg curl exercise. You can also lie on your back with your foot extended to a point several feet up on the wall. Then pull down and do an isometric contraction with a straight leg and hold that contraction for 8–10 seconds. Repeat the exercise 3–5 times. This "paw down" motion is similar to the Ralph Mann form drills and closely simulates that phase of the sprinting action.

Roller skates offer a unique method of training the muscle groups at the hip, knee, and ankle that are responsible for the driving force in sprinting (gluteals, hamstrings, quadriceps, and calf muscles). Four areas of conditioning are recommended that use skates:

- *Range of motion in all possible directions of hip-leg movement.* The legs should be moved in all directions. Begin by holding on to a chair while you complete 8–12 repetitions in all directions. Build up to 3 sets and emphasize flexibility.

- *Muscle endurance exercises for sprinting.* Move the legs back and forth with a slight bend at the knee. Using ankle weights or surgical tubing will provide the necessary loading. Complete 3 sets of 8–12 repetitions with as rapid a movement as possible with the load.

- *Speed endurance exercises.* High-speed back-and-forth movement is used for 10–30 seconds, working up to 30–60 seconds. You should gradually build up to 8–12 repetitions in sets of 4, resting 1.5–3 minutes between each set.

- *Overspeed skate training.* Hold on to a support and move the legs as fast as possible in a back-and-forth motion. Complete 3–5 sets of 8–12 repetitions with maximum rest (full recovery) between each set. When you have adjusted to the high-speed work, complete each set without holding on.

Table 3.7 Functional Strength Performance Standards

Level	Snatch	Clean	Clean and jerk	Power curl	Pull
I: Very poor	.50	.90	.90	.70	1.10
II: Poor	.70	1.10	1.10	.90	1.30
III: Average	.90	1.30	1.30	1.10	1.50
IV: Good	1.10	1.50	1.50	1.30	1.70
V: Excellent	1.30	1.70	1.70	1.50	1.90

Legs and back

Knee bend	Back one-quarter squat	Back one-half squat	Back three-quarters squat	Front squat	Dead squat	Good morning
	135°	90°	45°	45°		
I: Very poor	1.70	1.50	1.30	1.20		.30
II: Poor	2.00	1.80	1.60	1.40		.40
III: Average	2.30	2.10	1.90	1.60		.50
IV: Good	2.60	2.40	2.20	1.80		.60
V: Excellent	2.90	2.70	2.50	2.00		.70

(Cont.)

Table 3.7 (Cont.)

			Pushing (arms and shoulders)		
	Military	Incline	Bench	20-second bar dip	20-second push-ups
I: Very poor	.40	.50	.80	4 reps	11 reps
II: Poor	.60	.80	1.10	12 reps	19 reps
III: Average	.80	1.10	1.40	20 reps	27 reps
IV: Good	1.00	1.40	1.70	28 reps	35 reps
V: Excellent	1.20	1.70	2.70	36 reps	43 reps

(Numbers indicate % Body Weight; Weight × % = Weight Lifted).

Note. Female athletes should also use this table. For a more accurate interpretation of your performance, use the category that is one level above your score. For example, a snatch using .90 would be a rating of "Good" for the female athlete rather than "Average."

Step 3: Ballistics: Improve the Explosiveness of Your Throwing, Kicking, and Initial Movements

Sprinting at high speeds can provide much of the necessary short-term energy system development for most sports. However, most sports also require short bursts of speed, rapid changes in direction, explosive power delivery at impact, and instantaneous power reception at impact. Often, these tasks occur at the same time and, in fact, should not be isolated from the total action. Step 3 in the 7-Step Model isolates the qualities in some instances, but in others it integrates them into meaningful drills and exercises (Figure 3.7).

Many present-day systems fail to recognize the importance of joining yielding and resisting into a unified whole commonly called a *flow state*. Flowing, yielding, and resisting must become part of your athletic vocabulary if you are to understand how your energy and your opponent's energy can be used to your advantage.

Technically, there are three categories of ballistics (power delivery, impact, and flow):

Figure 3.7 Randy White works on explosive kicking and hitting movements.

- *Sending energy away from the body*. This includes throwing various objects, such as footballs, basketballs, baseballs, and medicine balls, and assorted weights.
- *Receiving energy from an outside source*. Any form of catching will develop the necessary sensitivity for receiving outside forces. Boxers have traditionally used medicine balls for training. The Dallas Cowboys have used the medicine ball body catch for years to toughen the body and, more important, to sensitize the neuromuscular system so that it responds instantly to impact.

Sample Ballistic Program (Power Impact)

The following simple program can easily be included into your daily training schedule in the preseason. The individual or partner program can be used as part of your warm-up or your cool-down.

Medicine Ball Throws

Equipment.   Use medicine balls, sandbags, or weights, weighing from 2 to 25 pounds. A good sandbag can be made from an inner tube of a car tire. Tie it off on one end and fill it with sand, then tie it off again after you have reached the desired weight.

Method.   The purpose of this drill is to develop power in all directions of movement. Individually, with a partner, or in a group, perform the following movements 8–10 times in each direction: (a) forward throw under-/overhand, (b) backward throw overhead, (c) side throw (left side and front, right side and front), and (d) side throw (left side and back, right side and back) (Figure 3.8).

Medicine Ball Catches

Equipment.   Use medicine balls or sandbags, weighing from 2 to 25 pounds.

Method.   The purpose of this drill is to develop the receiving skills of the body. Individually, with a partner, or in a group, perform 25–50 repetitions of each exercise. Individually, throw the ball in the air and catch it with your body; make sure that the ball contacts various parts of the body to get the maximum training effect. With a partner or in a group, add unexpected elements

Figure 3.8 Medicine ball throw.

by surprising your partner(s) with various speeds and directions; absorb the shock of the ball with various parts of the body.

Each new step you have taken thus far has helped forge the key that will unlock the treasures of the kingdom of speed. The last 4 steps in the 7-Step Model are the magical windows that will allow you access to future speed.

Step 4: Plyometrics: Bridge the Gap Between Strength and Power

The word *plyometric* is derived from the Greek word *pleythyein*, meaning *to increase*, or from the Greek roots *plio* and *metric*, meaning *more* and *measure*, respectively. Plyometric exercises involve powerful muscular contractions in response to the rapid, dynamic loading (stretching) of the involved muscles. The unusual progress and success of Russian sprinter Valeriy Borzov—100-meter gold medal winner (10.0 seconds) in the 1972 Olympic Games—is partially attributed to his use of plyometric exercises during the 6-year period prior to the games. Borzov progressed from a 100-meter time of 13.0 seconds at age 14 to 10.0 seconds at age 20. Although you may not show as dramatic an improvement as Borzov showed, hopping, jumping, bounding, leaping, skipping, ricocheting, swinging, and twisting are important parts of your speed improvement program.

Plyometric training is an excellent way to develop both strength and power in the muscles involved in sprinting. Many athletes have superior strength but cannot produce the needed power to sprint a fast 40-yard dash. Plyometric training is designed to bridge this gap between strength and power and to improve the explosive action of leaping from one foot to another, which we call sprinting.

Whether you know it or not, you apply the basic concept of plyometrics in almost every sport, for example, when you cock your wrist before hitting a forehand or a backhand in tennis, throw a football, throw or hit a baseball, shoot a basketball, or swing a golf club. The rapid stretching (loading) of these muscles activates a *muscle spindle reflex,* which sends a powerful stimulus to the muscles that causes them to contract faster and with more power. What you are doing is rapidly stretching a muscle group and then immediately contracting that same group. In simple terms, the loading or stretching action is sometimes called the *yielding* phase and the actual reflex contraction of the muscles the *overcoming* phase.

Rapid loading of the muscles (yielding phase) must occur just before the contraction phase of these same muscles. For example, when you jump from an elevated platform to the ground, your legs bend under the gravity force (kinetic energy) and an immediate reactive jump occurs. How much your legs bend depends on the gravity force and the stored energy that will be used to release the powerful contraction to jump. The yielding phase produces stored energy that is released during the overcoming phase by a powerful contraction.

Does this program sound complicated? It is really quite simple. To use plyometrics properly, you need to follow four simple guidelines:

- You must use plyometric exercises that result in "down time" (the time your feet are on the ground) that is less than the down time in actual sprinting. The faster a muscle is forced to lengthen, the greater the tension it exerts. Also, the closer the stretch of the muscle is to the contraction, the more violent the contraction. When you are jumping from boxes or bleachers, avoid hesitating after ground contact; the object is to be on the ground for as short a time as possible by shortening the span between contact and takeoff. Intensity is a key variable. Emphasize quickness and maximal effort on each repetition. Keep in mind that a greater reflex response occurs when the muscle is loaded rapidly.

- Although weights can be used to increase the resistance, too much weight (e.g., from a vest or ankle spats) may increase strength without much effect on power. Also, too much weight can make it impossible to jump explosively. Your body provides enough resistance; there is no need to add additional weight.

- Follow the proper technique on each repetition. In all exercises, emphasize a ''knee/thumbs-up'' position, which helps maintain your balance and centers the work load around your hips and legs. When using an upper-body exercise, emphasize proper follow-through. The key aspects of plyometric exercises are push-off, extension, and knee drive. Emphasize the quality rather than the quantity of each jump.

- Use 3–6 sets of 8–10 jumps with 1–2 minutes of rest between each set. Add one to two jumps per set for each workout. When your total number of jumps reaches 250, concentrate more on the quality of the jump and on increased explosive action.

Safety Precautions

We are seeing an increasing number of injuries (shin, knee, ankle, and lower back) among athletes who use plyometric training. In most cases these injuries are a direct result of too many workouts per week, too many jumps per workout, incorrect form, jumping on hard surfaces, and using plyometrics at too early an age or without the necessary leg strength. To reduce your chances of injury, follow these guidelines:

- Avoid plyometrics altogether if you are under age 13 or cannot leg press 2.5 times your body weight. Younger athletes (prepubescent) should not use plyometrics in their workouts. Although only limited evidence is available, the potential to damage joints is present.

- Warm up properly by using careful stretching exercises and a general warm-up consisting of walk-jog-stride-sprint cycles for at least half a mile before starting your plyometric workout.

- Jump only on soft, grassy areas or on gymnastic mats, never on asphalt or a gymnasium floor.
- Use heel cups if you are prone to heel bruises or heel soreness.
- Use plyometric exercises every other day and never on the same day that you weight train. Plyometrics should also be done at the end of your workout or practice program.

Plyometric Exercises

Many different types of exercises are used in various sports. For speed improvement, we are interested only in a few basic jumps that involve limited ground contact time. A number of common plyometric drills result in a down time 2–3 times longer than in the sprinting action. Although some of these drills are important because the down time is similar to that of the start and acceleration phases of the 40-yard dash, most of your routine should involve jumps with short down time. Figures 3.9–3.12 show some of the most important exercises for speed improvement.

Bounds

Double Leg Bound (Figure 3.9a)
From a standing broad jump position (half-squat stance, arms at sides, shoulders forward, back straight, and head up), thrust your arms forward as the knees and body straighten and the arms "reach for the sky."

Alternate Leg Bound (Figure 3.9b)
Place one foot slightly ahead of the other. Push off with your back leg, drive the lead knee up to the chest, and try to gain as much height and distance as possible. Continue by immediately driving with the other leg on landing.

Running Bound (Figure 3.9c)
Run forward, jumping as far as possible with each step. Emphasize height and a high knee lift and land with the center of gravity under you.

Lateral Bound (Figure 3.9d)
Assume a semisquat stance and push off the outside foot to propel yourself sideward. As soon as you land, drive off again in the opposite direction, emphasizing lateral distance.

Figure 3.9a Double leg bound.

Figure 3.9b Alternate leg bound.

Figure 3.9c Running bound.

Figure 3.9d Lateral bound.

Hops

Single-Leg Speed Hop (Figure 3.10)

Assume the position described above with one leg in a stationary flexed position. Emphasize height as in the double-leg speed hop.

Jumps

Double-Leg Speed Jump (Figure 3.11a)

From an upright position with your back straight, shoulders forward, and head up, jump upward as high as possible bringing your feet under your buttocks in a cycling motion at the height of the jump. Repeat the jump from the top of a grassy hill with a 3–4 degree slope, hopping down the hill for speed.

Squat Jump (Figure 3.11b)

From an upright position with your hands behind your head, drop downward to a half-squat position and immediately explode upward as high as possible. Repeat the sequence on landing, emphasizing maximum height.

Side Jump and Sprint (Figure 3.11c)

Stand to one side of a bench or tackling dummy with your feet together and pointing straight ahead. Jump back and forth over the bench for 4 to 10 repetitions. After landing on the last jump, sprint forward for 25 yards. Two players begin this exercise at the same time. The first one to complete the specified number of jumps and reach the finish line is the winner. Ten benches or cones can be set up 10 yards apart for 100 yards. Players perform 4 to 10 jumps and sprint to the next cone before repeating the jumps and sprinting again.

Swings

Sprint-Arm Action (Figure 3.12)

With a dumbbell (5 to 30 pounds) in each hand, perform 10 repetitions of the arm-sprinting action, stopping for 1 to 2 seconds and repeating for 10 more repetitions. Complete 6 to 10 sets.

Ricochets can also be used to improve foot and leg quickness. Stand facing the bottom of the bleacher steps with your feet together and arms to the sides. Rapidly move up every step as fast as possible, trying to be "light on your feet." You can use the same movement from the top of a 2–4-degree grassy hill by taking a series of short, rapid movements down the hill. Concentrate on being light on your feet.

Figure 3.10 Single leg speed hop.

Figure 3.11a Double leg speed jump.

Figure 3.11b   Squat jump.

Figure 3.11c Side jump and sprint.

Figure 3.12 Sprint arm action.

Number of Jumps Per Workout

To date it is unknown how many jumps give the best results. Coaches at various levels differ in terms of the number of repetitions, sets, and total jumps in a single workout. However, it is better to take too few jumps than to take too many. Ideally, the number of jumps should not exceed 75 in early workouts or 250 after 4 to 6 weeks of training.

Plan to use your plyometric program at the end of your workout twice weekly and early in the week, such as Monday and Wednesday. Vary the types of exercises by choosing from those shown in Figures 3.9–3.12. Follow the suggested number of jumps and sets shown in Table 3.8 below.

Table 3.8 Plyometric Workout and Progression

Type	Number of jumps	Sets	Rest intervals (min)	Progression
Bounds Double leg Alternate leg Running bound Lateral bound	8–10	1–2	1.5	Add 1 jump per workout until you reach 10. Return to 8 jumps and complete 2 sets. When you can complete 2 sets of 10 repetitions, stay at that level.
Hops Double-leg speed jump Single-leg speed hop	10–15	1–2	1	Progress as described above.
Jumps Squat jump Side jump and sprint	8–10	1–2	1	Progress as described above.
Ricochets Incline ricochet Decline ricochet	15–20	1–2	1	Progress as described above.
Swings Sprint-arm action	10–15	1–2	1	Progress as described above.

Note. On each workout, use only two plyometric exercises from each major group plus one skip. The minimum number of total jumps in early workouts using the lowest repetition number and 1 set (not including swings) is 97. The maximum number of total jumps in later workouts using the highest repetition number and 2 sets (not including swings) is 250.

Step 5: Sprint Loading:
Sprint Against Increasing Resistance

Although you probably do not have all the technical equipment that the Dallas Cowboys use for sprint-loaded training, you need not worry. Below are several simple methods that can be used by everyone.

Hill Sprinting

Most parts of the country provide suitable terrain for sprinting uphill. Although a wide range of grades can be used, it is recommended that the degree of incline allow you to run with good starting and sprinting form. A 10- to 30-yard incline of 2.5 to 10 degrees should be covered as fast as possible and be followed by a near-full-speed sprint of 20 to 80 yards at the same incline if the distance is available. These values have proven to be very effective for sprint-loaded programs at the Dallas Cowboy training facility. You should try to come as close as possible to these guidelines, although precise values are not absolutely necessary.

Stadium Stairs

Stadiums or other stairs can be used in the same manner as hill sprinting. Try to locate stairs that have the same approximate angles.

Weighted Sleds

Both expensive and inexpensive sleds are available (Figure 3.13). A spare tire with a rope and weighted belt can also be made at little cost. Metal and plastic models are also available that allow quick and easy weight changes. Regardless of the device you choose, make sure you use a load that allows proper form and high-speed sprinting. Too much weight will cause you to break form and will prevent explosive movements. Time yourself over various starting and sprinting distances of 5 to 40 yards using both a stationary and a flying start.

Figure 3.13 Weighted sled.

Diagnostic Power Trainer

This computerized machine of the future (Figure 3.14) provides instantaneous measurement and evaluation of power delivery in sport; a dream turning into a reality at Valley Ranch for the Dallas Cowboys. Preliminary work is being evaluated to determine how power is delivered by players as they run, block, and tackle. Power curves are providing the data by identifying errors, diagnosing problems, recognizing the cause of error, diagnosing conditioning faults, and specifying conditioning or special training to remedy the errors. Selecting productive training cycles is a critical part of this process.

The Diagnostic Power Trainer is so sensitive to the energy that a player exerts that major training breakthroughs will be made through its use. Decisions can be made about ground contact of each foot to see whether there is adequate power and balance between feet, prestoring of kinetic energy in the body segments, and intrastride sequencing of each limb for storing and exchanging energy in perfectly timed thrusts. This method will be available to athletes in the near future.

Figure 3.14   Diagnostic Power Trainer.

Sample Sprint-Loaded Program Recommendations

The best time point to include sprint-loaded training in your program is at the latter part of Wednesday's workout or later in Speed Week. There are two training objectives you need to consider in your program plan:

- *Power start*. This phase helps you get started in your run to near-maximum speed. Studies show that the length of your acceleration-power starts should be 60 to 80 yards, or 6 to 8 seconds. Peak power is attained at about .6 to .8 seconds (within 10 yards). Therefore, you should train peak power by doing starts that cover 10 to 20 yards. Six to 10 repetitions are recommended.
- *Power sprint*. This phase trains you to develop power at high speeds. The speed curves of sprinters show that deliverable power drops off as you move faster. The best way to train high-speed power is to do sprint-loaded work from a flying start, using incline sprints at maximum or near-maximum levels. Six to 10 repetitions for 10 to 80 yards should be used.

Table 3.9 is a sample sprint-loaded program for hill sprinting, stadium stair sprinting, and weighted sleds.

Table 3.9   Sprint-Loading Program Using Hill Sprinting, Stadium Stairs, or a Weighted Sled

Week	Repetitions	Pulling distance (yd)[a]	Rest (min)	Progression
1	3–5	15	2	Use power starts at three-quarters speed in hill and stadium sprinting or with no weight on the sled. Complete 2 sets.
2	3–5	20	2	Repeat above at maximum speed.
3	6–8	25	2	Repeat power starts above at maximum speed.
	3–5	30	2	Use power sprints at maximum speed in hill and stadium sprinting or with no weight on the sled. Complete 2 sets.
4	7–9	40	3	Repeat above power starts and power sprints; add weight to sled that allows you to sprint with good form. Complete 2 sets.
5	7–9	50	3	Repeat above workout. Add more weight. Complete 3 sets.
6–9	7–9	60	4	Repeat above workout. Add more weight each week. Complete 3 sets. Include one final run to exhaustion by continuing your sprint for as long as possible. Record the distance and try to improve your distance pull each week.

[a]Actual distance you are pulling the sled or sprinting uphill or up stadium steps.

Step 6: Sportspeed: Improve Your Sprinting Form and Speed Endurance

Form and speed endurance have been grouped together because both fit into the category of sporting speed. Although training varies somewhat depending on your sport, it is important for you to devote some workout time to each area.

Sprinting Form

Sprinting techniques vary from individual to individual, with so-called correct form generally being associated with champion sprinters. Remember that there is no perfect style for anyone of any body type. Because you are an individual, you must learn the ideals of form in theory and then adapt it to your own personal traits. This will give you the best results.

Proper sprinting form is not a natural act. Nine out of 10 individuals from the elementary school through the college years have faulty styles. Eliminating faulty habits requires special attention. On the other hand, *we have not seen small changes in sprinting form result in large improvements in sprinting speed, unless these changes were in the start* (including the first 15 yards) from a 3-point stance or the track position. Although form is important, it receives far too much attention by many athletes and coaches at the expense of other training programs. We will briefly cover key points that will help you improve your starting technique and eliminate gross form errors during the sprinting phase. Two 15- to 20-minute form-training sessions per week with your coach or friend should be enough time to make a difference.

Starting Form for the 40-Yard Dash

The 40-yard dash is already the single most important test used by football coaches to evaluate players for various positions, to choose team members, to offer scholarships, and to keep or retain players. The 40-yard dash and its variations are rapidly becoming equally as common in baseball (home to first, home to second, home to third, 60-yard dash), basketball (20-yard dash), and soccer (flying 40).

The success of your future in sports depends on your time in a short distance such as 20 to 60 yards. In spite of this fact, no test is more poorly completed by athletes in all sports than the stationary 40-yard dash. Athletes of all ages and from all levels of competition have been known to have poor starting form. Errors in foot spacing, push-off, forward lean, and arm thrust are common. These are errors that few track sprinters ever make. Team-sport athletes rarely take the time to work with their track coach on starting technique in spite of the fact that the first 15 yards of a 40-yard dash are the most important of the entire race.

The 16-point program that follows was prepared for team-sport athletes and points out the areas where most of the faulty techniques have been identified in our speed clinics and camps from 1971 to 1987. Remember that some suggestions are made only for the 40-yard dash and do not apply to sporting speed, or situations in an actual game when you would be accelerating from a stationary position. These suggestions assume that you are moving in a straight line, want to get there as fast as possible, and will have no interference from an opponent. Mastering these suggestions on the starting phase will help improve your time.

- Learn the medium track start and adapt it to the 3-point stance (Figure 3.15) if you are a football player and feel comfortable only in the three-point stance; otherwise, use the 4-point track stance (Figure 3.16) when sprinting a 40-yard dash for time. Work with your track coach until you are comfortable with every phase of the medium start. Place the front foot (95% of elite male sprinters place the left foot forward) 14 to 21 inches behind the starting line with the knee of your rear leg almost even with the toe of your front foot. If your front foot is too close to the starting line, too much of your body weight will rest on it, making it impossible for the angle of the leg at the knee to reach the desired 90 degrees. Assume a relaxed position with weight back and arms, neck, and back relaxed. Arms slant backward from the starting line, and the head is down with eyes looking at the ground. When you are ready, slowly shift your weight forward, then up. Lift the front knee 6 to 8 inches with the legs almost parallel to the ground. The buttocks should be about 3 to 5 inches higher than the shoulders. A slow shift forward places tension on the hands for a limited time only. Drive the left arm forward and up, bent 90 degrees

Figure 3.15   3-point football stance using the medium start with the knee on the ground (r) and final set position with weight forward (l).

at the elbow, as you drive the right arm back only to the hip, then thrust forward. The head is now up with the eyes focused 15 to 20 yards ahead. The drive angle is low and forward. The lead knee is high with the first step touching 16 to 19 inches beyond the starting time. Steps are now long, knee lift remains high, and arms are thrust long and forward.

- Practice the 4-point track stance until it feels comfortable. This technique allows you to support your weight better in the forward-lean position and is superior to a 3-point football stance for the 40-yard dash.
- Place considerable weight on your hand. Everyone knows you are going forward; there is no need to keep the weight back and cheat yourself out of valuable starting time. The best times are recorded when an athlete complains of ''stumbling'' out of the blocks. When acceleration is the greatest, the forward body lean should also be the greatest for best results. Your trunk controls the body's center of gravity; the further forward you place your center of gravity in relation to your support, the greater your forward lean. Forward lean also helps keep you from straightening up too soon.

Figure 3.16   4-point stance using the medium start with the knee on the ground (r) and final set position with weight forward (l).

- Lean forward until your shoulders are over the line while the right knee is still on the ground. It is easier to hold your weight over the line with the knee down. Raise your hips about 3 to 5 inches higher than the shoulders to assume the ''set'' position.
- Focus your head and eyes downward, looking no more than 6 to 8 yards ahead of the field.
- Push off with both feet simultaneously and with equal thrust. All good track sprinters exert force against both the front and the back blocks. Football players in the traditional 3-point stance make the common error of stepping forward with the rear leg and applying almost no thrust with the back foot. This bad habit slows your start and results in a poor 40-yard-dash time. A good track athlete, on the other hand, exerts more force on the rear block even though the lead leg is in contact with the block longer and contributes more to block velocity. No athlete more clearly pushed off both feet than did Ben Johnson of Canada on his way to a 9.83 world record in the 100-meter dash in Rome, Italy, on August 31, 1987. Placing his arms much wider than shoulder width, Ben ''jumped'' out of the blocks to obtain a quick lead on Olympic medal winner Carl Lewis (who

tied the previous world record of 9.93), a lead Ben Johnson held until the end of his world record run. It is much easier to learn to push off both feet from the medium stance with the feet fairly close together. When the feet are too far apart, a push-off with both feet is awkward and inefficient. Strive to obtain a full extension of the hip, knee, and ankle joints. This guarantees a forceful, simultaneous thrust with both legs.

- Your first movement forward is with the arms. Initiate an aggressive arm drive off the starting line (left arm drives forward as the right arm moves backward).

- A correct start involves complex motor skills that must be implanted in long-term memory if they are to be performed automatically. The best way for you to attain this goal is to perform hundreds, perhaps thousands, of correct starts. Short daily practice sessions of 15–20 minutes on this important phase will yield positive results in 3–4 weeks.

- Maintain the ''hold'' position for only a very short period of time to reduce the strain on your hands. After your hand and foot placements are perfected, raise your tail to move your weight forward, then start immediately. The procedure will be effective when the timer allows you to start when you want to.

- On natural turf, dig two small holes in the ground to increase traction for both feet to push off.

- Stay low for the first 6 to 8 yards. Straightening up too fast reduces natural forward momentum. Ask your coach to analyze your first 10 to 15 yards to make certain that you are not straightening up too soon, that you have the proper weight distribution, and that you are following acceptable form during the acceleration phase.

- Use vigorous arm movement the first 10 yards; continue to work the arms hard throughout the 40 yards. ''Lazy'' arms will affect your time.

- Most 40-yard tests allow you to start when you want to. The timer then reacts to your first muscular movement. If your start was poor, stop sprinting and do not complete the run. Return to the starting line and try again.

- While it may be unethical to outguess the timer by shifting your weight and starting before he or she is ready, you also do not want the timer outguessing you. Leaving too soon will only result in a retest. Leaving too late will give you a poor time.

- Sprint 5 to 8 yards past the timer rather than using the "lunge" method. In most cases, a finish line will not be used.
- Ask for another trial if you feel you had a bad run. Your career is too important to be judged on only one 40-yard dash.

The Sprinting Action

Remember that sprinting is merely a series of leaps. If you run 100 meters in 12 seconds, for example, you have foot/ground contact for about 5 seconds and are in the air for 7 seconds. Unfortunately, straight running, rhythm, bounce, relaxation, smoothness, and mechanically sound upper- and lower-body movements are needed to take these leaps with maximum efficiency. You must master acceptable form from the start to the finish by studying, by experimentation, and by adapting techniques of form to your body traits.

We will identify some of the more common form errors and suggest simple methods of correction (Table 3.10). Again, it must be pointed out that variations in form exist from one athlete to another and that small changes may do little to improve your time. Correcting major faults, on the other hand, can cut valuable tenths of a second off your time.

Form Training

Form training is difficult. Over 1,000 different drills have been used in the past by track coaches. Fortunately, only a few are needed to improve form, providing these drills meet three standards: (a) Form drills must be highly specific to the activity to which training is aimed in terms of speed and down time (ground contact time). (b) Drills must involve the same range of motion as sprinting. (c) Drills must involve similar strength/power demands. Drills used in the past have not applied these concepts. Ground contact time (down time) in form-training drills used in the past is 2 to 4 times longer than that used in sprinting, similar to down time in the start and the first 3 to 5 yards. Remember that you need to learn how to sprint, not just run, faster.

It is interesting to note that the stride lengths of elite and average sprinters do not differ by much; however, stride-rate differences are great with elite sprinters, who take more steps per second than do average sprinters. Better sprinters also sprint with slightly less forward body lean than do slower sprinters. High knee lift is

Table 3.10 Common Form Errors and Their Corrections

Common areas of difficulty	Corrections
Arm action	Practice loose, swinging movements from a standing position. Swing entire arm from the shoulders. Thumbs should brush the thighs. Increase arm speed, flex elbows more, loosely cup the hands, and brush thumbs against the sides. Repeat while moving forward high on the toes.
Hands too low	Place tape around the wrist and over the neck.
Hands moving too far forward	Practice arm swing to contact coach's hands when standing behind the runner.
Hands outside line of elbows	Sprint while holding a stick in both hands with proper spacing. Use tape on both wrists at proper spacing.
Body lean	Practice sprinting with eye concentration on a fixed spot, either high or low, depending on the problem. Discuss mechanics of proper lean at maximum speed. After acceleration (25–42 yd.), concentrate on running erect.
Incorrect head alignment	Same as above.
Limited foot bounce	Walk forward high on toes using proper arm action, keeping body weight as low as possible, and bouncing the knee forward from the foot. Stand on one foot and bounce the opposite foot up and down on the sole as rapidly as possible.
Unnecessary pounding into the ground	Practice running as lightly as possible with correct foot-ground contact.
Incorrect knee-leg action	Practice running upstairs two at a time and running along the beach in shallow water.
Striding:	
Overstriding	Practice running along the beach in shallow water. Avoid placing the lead foot too far beyond the center of gravity. The foot hits slightly in front of the center of gravity; however, it should be

(Cont.)

Table 3.10 (Cont.)

Common areas of difficulty	Corrections
	moving to the rear on contact to avoid overbraking.
Understriding	Concentrate on complete extension of the hip and knee joint at ground contact and complete knee pickup of the recovery leg. See section on stride training.
Upper-arm tension	Cocontraction of opposing muscle groups causes tension. Unclench the fist and generate tension in the thumb with pressure against the index finger.
Neck/facial tension	Roll out the lower lip and yawn.

another important trait because it permits longer extension to the ground. A final key factor is the recommended quadricep/hamstring strength ratio guidelines of 1:.75 (hamstrings should be 75% of quadriceps) discussed in chapter 2. The hamstrings are the weak link in sprinting and should be as strong as you can possibly make them. The pull-down is controlled by hamstring strength and power.

Key Form Drills for Your Workout. Ralph Mann—former Olympic silver medalist in the 400-meter hurdles and current speed improvement specialist—evaluated over 1,000 drills for down time, proper technique, and duplication of skills. The bounding, sprinting, and workout drills that follow have been successfully used by Mann in his training program to improve speed in short distances.

Bounding Drills. These drills are designed to develop the explosive leg power required in starting. They are stressful enough to be a workout, or they can be part of a workout. They are *not* designed to be warm-up or cool-down drills.

Straight bounding. Beginning from a slow jog, try to bound as high into the air as possible using a running form that emphasizes a high knee lift. Land on the opposite leg and continue the bounding down the field. The intensity of this drill is controlled by altering the height and the number of repetitions. For beginners and heavier players, the height of the bound should be limited and the number of bounds kept at no more than four with each leg. As your experience and training progress, you can increase the height and the number of repetitions (Figure 3.17).

Outside bounding. This drill is similar to straight bounding, except that the foot is placed laterally outside the normal landing position, and the body is projected laterally as well as up and forward (Figure 3.18). The drill should be used after you have had experience with straight bounding.

Inside bounding. This drill is similar to outside bounding except that the foot is placed laterally inside the normal landing position, and the body is projected laterally as well as up and forward (Figure 3.19). This drill should be used after you have had experience with straight bounding.

Sprinting Drills.   The following drills are designed to develop the mechanics, strength, and power needed to produce maximum performance in sprinting. They are designed for use while you warm up before a workout. The length and difficulty of each drill can be altered to any desired distance and intensity.

Butt kickers. From a jog, the lower leg is allowed to swing back and to bounce off the buttocks. The upper leg should not move much. Place emphasis on allowing (not forcing) the heel to come to the butt (Figure 3.20).

Wall slide. From a jog, the action is the same as for butt kickers except that the heel of the recovery leg must not travel in back of the body. Imagine a wall of glass running down the back, and do not allow the heel to break the glass. This action will produce knee lift without forcing the action. As in butt kickers, when done properly, the heel will bounce off the butt (Figure 3.21).

Pawing. From a jog, reach out and pull the ground toward you in a pawing action. Like a cat, keep all effort in front of the body. Do not drive off the ground (Figure 3.22).

Start and sprint. From a stationary position, start quickly, and feel the power being applied behind the body. Ten yards out, quickly shift from running in back of the body to sprinting in front of the body. This should emphasize the difference between starting technique (behind the body) and sprinting technique (in front of the body).

Quick feet drill. From a jog, increase your stride rate such that you take as many steps as possible in a 10-yard interval. Jog for 10 yards

Figure 3.17 Straight bounding.

Figure 3.18 Outside bounding.

Figure 3.19 Inside bounding.

Figure 3.20 Butt kickers.

Figure 3.21 Wall slide.

Figure 3.22 Pawing.

Figure 3.23 Quick feet.

and repeat. Emphasis should be placed on quick turnover with the legs moving in front, not behind or under, the body (Figure 3.23).

Workout Drills.   These drills were designed to perform as a workout or as part of a workout. Typically, 3 sets of each drill are performed. It is important that each of these drills be started on the toes and an effort made to remain in this position during the drill.

Cycling. Leaning against a wall, bar, or any support, one leg is cycled through in a sprinting manner. Emphasis is placed on keeping the leg from extending in back of the body, allowing the foot to kick the butt during recovery, then pawing the ground to complete the action (Figure 3.24). Ten cycles with each leg make up 1 set.

Butt kickers. Same as butt kickers in the warm-up drills except that the emphasis should be more on quickness. Ten kicks with each leg make up 1 set.

Down and offs. From a high knee position, the emphasis is to decrease your foot/ground contact by hitting the ground with the ball of the foot and getting off as quickly as possible. In turn, the effort on the ground should bounce the leg up into the high knee position (Figure 3.25). Ten down and offs with each leg make up 1 set.

Pull-throughs. Extending the leg in front of the body (like a hurdler), the leg is then brought down and through ground contact in a power motion (Figure 3.26). Ten pull-throughs with each leg make up 1 set.

Stick drill. Twenty sticks (18 to 24 inches in length) are placed 18 inches apart on a grass surface. Athletes sprint through the sticks as fast as possible, touching one foot down between each. High knee lift and quick ground contact are emphasized. Coaches can time athletes by starting a stopwatch when the foot contacts the ground between the first and the second stick and by stopping the watch when a foot contacts the ground after passing the final stick. One completion of the drill makes up 1 set.

African dance. While running forward, raise each leg to the side of the body as in hurdling, and tap each heel with the hand (Figure 3.27). A 10-yard run equals 1 set. Start this drill easily and gradually build up the intensity.

Drum major. While running forward, rotate the leg inward to the mid-line of the body, and tap the heel at the mid-line (Figure 3.28). A 10-yard run equals 1 set.

Figure 3.24 Cycling.

Figure 3.25 Down and offs.

Figure 3.26 Pull-throughs.

Figure 3.27 African dance.

Figure 3.28 Drum major.

Speed Endurance Training

As we discussed in chapter 2, speed endurance training will not help you take a faster or longer step. It will, however, prevent you from slowing down late in the game, at the end of a long sprint, or after sprinting several times with little rest in between. You have seen many examples of poor speed endurance in different sports. A halfback is tackled from behind by a slower player. A sprinter is passed in the final 10 meters of a race. A baseball player ''runs out of steam'' and is tagged out at home. A basketball player is beaten to the ball by a slower player. All these are examples of poor speed endurance, which causes a player either to slow down or to fail to accelerate as fast as normal due to fatigue. In most sports a player is expected to make repeated bursts of speed. Ideally, the fourth or fifth sprint is run as fast as the first. This is often not the case due to poor speed endurance. By becoming well conditioned for speed endurance, you will have several advantages in your sport: (a) repeated short sprints can be made with minimum rest all at the same high speed, (b) maximum speed is reached more quickly, and (c) maximum speed is held for a longer distance before slowing occurs.

High levels of speed endurance provide you with a fresh start on each short sprint. Speed endurance training is a vital phase for athletes in team sports such as football, basketball, and baseball. It is the phase that can give you the edge.

Speed endurance is easy to improve. You only need to sprint short distances 2 to 3 times per week and keep a record of how many repetitions you sprinted, how far you sprinted, and how much recovery time you took between each repetition. The rest is easy. On each workout, you simply increase the sprint distance and decrease the recovery time between each repetition. In a period of 6 to 8 weeks, your speed endurance will be higher.

The following guidelines will help you understand how to devise the best program for your sport:

- Sprinting (up to 200 meters) is 90% to 95% anaerobic, and training should reflect this percentage. Aerobic training (lap running and jogging) should occupy only a small portion of your training regimen. Improved aerobic conditioning has little or no effect on speed in short distances. Too much distance running in the preseason has been shown to decrease speed in short distances.

- Maximum sprints for short durations (10 to 60 seconds) should be used.
- Rest periods of a few minutes should follow each maximum effort.
- All-out sprints—covering approximately the same or greater distances than those normally sprinted in your sport, football, 20 to 60 yards; basketball, 10 to 30 yards; and baseball, 30 to 120 yards—should be used.
- A 1-minute maximum-effort sprint followed by 4 to 5 minutes of rest before repeating the effort improves speed endurance. Repetitive 400-meter runs in 60 to 75 seconds followed by a 4- to 5-minute rest period are also an effective technique.

Pickup Sprints

Pickup sprints are an easy, effective training program to improve speed endurance for football, baseball, and basketball. Pickup sprints involve a gradual increase from a jog to a striding pace, then to a maximum-effort sprint. A 1:1 ratio of the distance and recovery walk that follows each repetition should be used. For example, you may jog 25 yards, stride 25, sprint 25, and end that repetition with a 25-yard walk. The walk or slow jog should allow some recovery prior to the next repetition. This jog-stride-sprint-recovery cycle tends to develop speed endurance and reduce your chances of muscle injury in cold weather. The cycle is an example of early-season training, and the exact number of repetitions depends on your conditioning level. As you improve, the distance is lengthened, with late-season pickup sprints reaching segments of 120 yards.

New Zealand athletes use a routine similar to pickup sprints that involves a series of four 50-meter sprints at near-maximum speed (6 to 7 seconds) per 400-meter lap, jogging for 10 to 12 seconds after each sprint, and completing the 400-meter run in 64 to 76 seconds. Athletes have performed as many as 50 sprints (12.5 x 440) with little reduction in speed on any repetition.

The majority of speed endurance work for athletes in football, basketball, and baseball should involve segments of 25- to 50-yard sprints because the object is to train the fast-twitch (white) fiber and improve both conditioning and speed. Sprinting longer dis-

Table 3.11 Pickup-Sprint Training Program

Week	Workout item	Repetitions	Rest interval
1	Jog 25 yards, stride 25 yards (three-quarters speed), sprint and walk 25 yards	3–5 (add 1 per workout)	No rest between repetitions; walking phase serves as recovery
2	Jog 25 yards, stride 25 yards (three-quarters speed), sprint 25 yards and walk 25 yards	6–8 (add 1 per workout)	Same
3	Jog 50, stride 50, sprint 50, walk 50	3–5 (add 1 per workout)	Same
4	Jog 75, stride 75, sprint 75, walk 75	3–5 (add 1 per workout)	Same
5	Jog 75, stride 75, sprint 75, walk 75	6–8 (add 1 per workout)	Same
6	Jog 75, stride 75, sprint 75, walk 75	Maximum possible	Same

Note. If the workout is not strenuous enough, lengthen the distances, working up to 120-, 150-, 220-, and 300-yard cycles.

tances (50, 75, 100, or 125 yards) can be used occasionally as the final 1 to 3 repetitions of a workout.

You can retest yourself in the 120-yard dash and compare your flying 40 time to your 80- to 120-yard time to check your speed endurance. Another check test involves completing 6 consecutive 40-yard dashes at 30-second intervals and then comparing the drop-off. Ideally, none of the timed 40s should be more than .2 seconds off your best effort. Assume the 3- or the 4-point stance at the starting line and have a coach or friend time you in the 40-yard dash. Now walk forward 10 yards slowly and begin your second timed 40 when exactly 30 seconds have elapsed. Repeat this procedure once up and once down the area until you have completed 6 timed 40-yard dashes with a 30-second rest between each.

You are now ready to move on to the seventh and final step in the 7-Step Model for speed improvement: overspeed training.

Step 7: Overspeed Training: Take Faster Steps Than Ever Before

This is the seventh and final step of your speed improvement program. It is also the most fun. With overspeed training, you may actually run a 40-yard dash faster than Ben Johnson, Carl Lewis, or Willie Gault. The feeling of raw power and speed is very exciting. If you use overspeed training correctly, you will be amazed at the results.

There are four methods of overspeed training: (a) downhill sprinting, (b) high-speed cycling, (c) towing with surgical tubing, and (d) towing with the Sprint Master. With proper use, athletes have improved their 40-yard-dash time by as much as .6 seconds. Track athletes in the 100-meter dash have improved their times more than .8 seconds. Plan to stay with the program a minimum of 8 weeks.

Downhill Sprinting

You can use downhill sprinting without purchasing any special equipment. Athletes have improved their 40-yard-dash times by .4 seconds with proper use of downhill sprinting. You must, however, locate a 20- to 70-yard slope of no more than 2.5 to 3.0 degrees. Consult your coach for suggestions. A 3-degree slope requires only a slight decline. If the slope is too great, body lean decreases, and you will contact the ground too far in front of the body, producing a braking effect. As a result, a forceful push-off is nearly impossible. Ideally, the area should have a 15- to 20-yard flat area followed by a 20- to 70-yard, 2.5- to 3.0-degree downhill slope and end with a 15- to 80-yard flat area. You should try to reach near-maximum speed before reaching the downhill area, sprint downhill for at least 20 yards at superhigh speed, and then hold the increased speed for 20 yards on the flat area.

Follow the program shown in Table 3.12 and pay close attention to the rest or recovery period between each repetition.

Downhill Sprint Variation

Remember to emphasize stride rate—a faster leg turnover—during the overspeed phase by shortening your stride length slightly. This will reduce the tendency of breaking on each step and will help develop a faster step. Accelerate down the hill for about 15 to 20 yards, then slightly shorten the length of your stride and take 13 steps as fast as you can. Allow a sufficient relaxed recovery period before the next repetition. Do 6 to 10 repetitions.

High-Speed Stationary Cycling

During high-speed cycling, wind resistance, gravity, and body weight are eliminated to allow you to complete more revolutions (similar to steps in sprinting) per second than you are capable of doing in the sprinting action. This overspeed technique should be used with one other method—towing, or downhill sprinting. Preliminary evidence indicates that high-speed cycling may increase your stride rate. Follow the program shown in Table 3.12.

Table 3.12 Downhill Sprinting and Cycling Program

Week	Repetitions	Acceleration distance	Overspeed distance[a]	Repetitions	Rest interval (min)
1	2–3	10–15 yd (1.5–2 sec)	20–25 yd (2–2.5 sec)	Add 1–2 per workout	2
2	4–6	15–20 yd (2–2.5 sec)	20–25 yd (1.5–2.5 sec)	Add 1 each workout	2.5
3	7–9	20–25 yd (2.5–3 sec)	20–25 yd (1.5–2.5 sec)	Add 1 each workout	3
4	9–10	20–25 yd (2.5–3 sec)	20–25 yd 1.5–2.5 sec)	Add 1 each workout	3.5–4
5	Avoid increasing the number of repetitions beyond 10; merely repeat the workout in Week 4. Be certain you are fully recovered after each repetition.				

[a]Overspeed distance is the actual distance (or time) you are sprinting downhill or pedaling at high speeds.

Towing

Towing athletes behind automobiles, motor scooters, and motor-cycles is not a new approach to the improvement of speed. In 1956, towing was used to train Olympic medal winner Al Lawrence, who held on to a rigid bar attached to a car 4 times per week for distances of 100 to 600 yards. In the 1960s it was successfully used in Australia to reduce the 100-meter-dash time of one subject who held on to the side of a tram car. In the United States, a pacing machine (a tow bar and handle attached to the rear bumper of an automobile) was used in 1961. Young runners increased their stride length considerably (average of 6 inches) and improved their 100-yard-dash time from an average of 10.5 to 9.9 seconds. In 1976, a 4-station tow bar at-tached to an automobile was used to improve 40-yard-dash times with a flying start. Towing has been a regular part of our speed camps since 1970 and ''overspeed'' training an important part of our training programs to improve 40-yard-dash times.

Towing produces higher stride rates and increases stride length more effectively than downhill sprinting. It also will improve your 40-yard-dash time more than other overspeed-training techniques. Do not be alarmed if you experience muscle soreness 1–2 days after your first towing session. Towing is demanding and will recruit muscle fibers that you are not accustomed to using. You can choose from two unique methods: towing with surgical tubing or towing with the Sprint Master.

Towing with Surgical Tubing

Surgical tubing can force you to take faster and longer steps and complete a 40-yard dash at world-record speed simply by providing you with a slight pull throughout your sprint. A 20- to 25-foot piece of elastic tubing is attached to your waist by a belt. The opposite end can be attached to another athlete or to a stationary object such as a tree or a goalpost to allow you to work out alone. You now back up to stretch the tubing slightly and run at three-fourths speed with the pull until you learn to adjust and keep your balance. After 4 to 5 practice runs, you should be ready for the full ride. You now back up about 25 to 30 yards before sprinting at high speed with the pull. Stationary runs from a 3-point start can also be made. Athletes in our speed clinics and camps have completed 3.58-second sta-tionary 40-yard dashes when being pulled with surgical tubing.

Training Suggestions. Surgical tubing allows you to train anytime, with or without a partner. A number of different drills can be used:

- Attach the tubing to a goal post. Within 3 trials, back up an extra 5 to 8 yards each trial to increase the pull as you adjust. Repeat this drill, emphasizing a high knee lift.
- Choose a faster athlete and race him or her while you are being towed. You will be amazed at how fast you are sprinting.
- To do the two-person drill, attach one end of the tubing to your waist and the other to your partner's back. Have your partner sprint 25 to 30 yards ahead against the resistance, then stop. You now sprint toward your partner in your overspeed run. Continue up and down the field.
- Repeat the above with both runners sprinting backward.
- To do the quick feet drill, measure one of your strides before placing 20 sticks at a distance 2 to 3 feet shorter than your stride. Repeat Drill 1, emphasizing rapid stride frequency.
- Allow the tubing to pull you at approximately .5 seconds faster than your best 40-yard-dash time. It takes only a slight pull to produce this effect. Place two marks 40 yards apart and have someone time you as you are being towed.

Follow the overspeed-training program (Table 3.13) 2 to 3 times per week (every other day) during the preseason and 1 to 2 times per week during the in-season.

Safety Precautions for Surgical Tubing. Using surgical tubing can be dangerous. Adequate supervision is recommended at all times. Tubing can break if stretched too far, and belts can come loose if they are carelessly fastened. Follow these safety tips carefully:

- Inspect the tubing before your first run each workout by letting the tubing slide through your hand as you back up. Any rough marks should be carefully examined. If a nick is detected, discard and replace with a new tubing.
- Inspect the knot on both belts and retie them if they are not tight or appear to be coming loose.

Table 3.13 Overspeed Training Program Using Surgical Tubing or the Sprint Master

Week	Repetitions	Overspeed distance (yd)[a]	Rest interval (min)	Progression
1	3–5	20	2	Three-quarter-speed runs only to acclimate
2	3–5	20	2	Maximum speed
3	5–7	25	3	Maximum speed
4	7–9	25	3	Maximum speed
5	7–9	35	3	Maximum speed
6–9	7–9	35	3.5	Maximum speed with 1-lb ankle spats or 5-lb weighted vest for 1–2 repetitions

[a]The actual distance you are sprinting at superhigh speeds (distance that the tubing or the Sprint Master is pulling).

- After you attach the belt to your waist, tie a knot with the remaining portion to make certain it cannot come loose.
- Avoid stretching the tubing more than 4–5 times its length.
- Avoid standing with the tubing fully stretched for more than 1 to 2 seconds. It is during this stretched phase that knots come loose.
- Use shoes without spikes the first several workouts until you have fully adjusted to the high speeds.
- Warm up properly. Stretch thoroughly and use a sequence of walk-jog-stride-sprint (20- to 25-yard segments) for a quarter to a half a mile.
- Use surgical tubing on soft grassy areas only.

Towing with the Sprint Master

Following a summer speed camp at Virginia Commonwealth University in Richmond, Virginia, in 1981, there was frustration over the problems with the use of a motor scooter to tow athletes at superhigh speeds. It was then that Dr. Dintiman indicated the

Figure 3.29 Bill Bates with the Sprint Master.

need for a motorized device that could be attached to a wall and used indoors or outdoors and that was capable of towing athletes at high, regulated speeds. John Dolan, who assisted in the speed camp, was immediately enthusiastic. With a highly mechanical friend, Michael Watkins, he made more than 20 prototypes before the Sprint Master was perfected. The Sprint Master is by far the most refined and practical method of towing athletes on a football field or in the gymnasium (Figure 3.29). No automobile, motor scooter, or motorcycle is needed. The machine is precisely engineered to pull athletes at speeds faster than any human can sprint without assistance. It attaches to the goalposts of a football field or to the wall of a gymnasium and provides controlled, variable speed for each athlete. This practical device is safe and eliminates the cumbersome, dangerous use of a vehicle. (For information on the Sprint Master, write to NASE, Box 35111, Richmond, VA 23235.)

The Sprint Master allows you full and proper use of your arms while you are towed at speeds of .5 to 1 seconds faster than your best 40-yard dash with a flying start. The following steps are used to start an overspeed program with the Sprint Master:

1. Use the workout schedule (Table 3.13) 2 to 3 times per week (every other day) in the preseason immediately after your warm-up or stretching routine, before you are fatigued from any other phase of your workout. During the season, follow the workout schedule 1 to 2 times per week to maintain your improved stride rate, stride length, and speed.

2. Your coach or friend should pull you at approximately .5 seconds faster than your best flying 40-yard-dash time. The operator quickly learns how to judge pace and can group athletes of similar speed together. It is also quite simple to place two marks 40 yards apart and time runners as they are being pulled. The set screw on the machine can then be fixed at the proper speed.

3. When you are being pulled, grasp the tow-rope handles and accelerate slowly for 10 to 15 yards. The Sprint Master will then exert its proper pull as you reach full speed and will continue to pull you for 20 to 25 yards, which at high speed is sufficient; longer distances tend to produce fatigue and cause you to lose your balance.

4. Practice the art of letting go of the tow-rope handles if you lose your balance. On an athletic field, especially in full football gear, a high-speed fall and a roll is generally safe. In using the Sprint Master in 4 years of speed camps, very few runners fall at any towing speed.

5. The full 2–4 minute rest period should be used between each repetition.

Operating the Sprint Master is easily learned and is described precisely in a brochure. Speeds can be individually determined for each athlete, and the pull can be made by the operator safely and accurately. In the Chicago Bear training camp, one runner completed a 2.9-second flying 40-yard dash (equivalent to a 3.6 or 3.7 stationary 40-yard dash and faster than Carl Lewis) while being towed with the Sprint Master. Chicago Bear coaches who timed the runner were surprised at the results.

Advanced Overspeed Training Techniques

A number of effective overspeed variations have been tested in our camps and clinics. These advanced methods are designed only for older, mature athletes who meet the leg strength standard (2.5 times body weight) described in chapter 2. After the first 2 weeks of adjustment, four different types of towing should be used in each session:

- Towing under complete control with proper sprinting form for 2 to 3 repetitions
- Towing out of control at superhigh speed with no concern for form for 1 to 2 repetitions
- Towing with a shortened stride for 2 to 3 repetitions at high speed while you consciously shorten your stride to increase stride rate greatly
- Sprint-loaded towing for 2 to 3 repetitions at high speed with weight added to the body (2 to 4 pounds—heavy hands or a 5-pound weighted vest).

General Safety Precautions

Warm up thoroughly before using any type of overspeed training. Take overspeed training seriously, and pay attention to the suggestions in each specific type to avoid muscle or equipment-related injuries that may occur due to horseplay or carelessness. Tow only on a soft, grassy area. Inspect the area for broken glass and other objects.

Overspeed training is the final step in the 7-Step Model. It is also the most demanding and the most effective. When it is used correctly with the previous 6 steps, results are often quite surprising.

Tips for Making Your Overspeed Training Program a Success

- Remember that you are trying to take faster and longer steps than ever before, not to improve your conditioning level for short sprints (see the speed endurance discussion in Step 6). You must therefore pay close attention to the rest period between each repetition. You should be fully recovered before completing the next repetition.
- Use overspeed training every other day (Monday/Wednesday/Friday) and no more than 3 times per week in the preseason and 2 times per week during the in-season period.
- Always use overspeed training in the beginning of your workout, immediately after stretching and general warm-up. You can only take ultrafast steps and long steps when you are free

from fatigue. Avoid any type of overspeed training after you are fatigued from drills, calisthenics, scrimmage, weight training, or plyometrics.

• Be patient and progress slowly. On your first workout, sprint only 3 times at three-quarters speed, 4 times 2 days later, and 5 times on your third workout of the first week. From the second to the ninth week you should progress in a similar fashion.

Why does overspeed training work? Many experts feel that overspeed methods actually train the nervous system. After a number of weeks of high-speed work, the nervous system permits you to take those faster steps without any assistance. Although this is only a theory, research clearly shows that the number of steps you take per second will improve following 4 to 8 weeks of overspeed work.

Chapter 4

Designing Your Own Personal Program

Life always gets harder near the summit.
—Friedrich Nietzsche

You now have everything you need to improve your speed. You have been tested, your scores have been evaluated, you have studied the speed improvement areas critical to your sport, and you have learned the 7-Step Model. You are now ready to begin your program. Before you do, let us review the purposes of each key training program to establish a logical order for each of your workouts. It is necessary to follow this order carefully to get the full benefits of the program and to avoid injury and overtraining. Hopefully, your coach will consider a similar order during the in-season period.

Flexibility training or stretching exercises and *formal warm-up* (actual jogging, striding, and light sprinting) have very little conditioning value. Their main contribution is to increase range of motion, to help prevent injuries, and to warm the body in preparation for the more vigorous parts of your program. Warm-up is important and should be completed before your workout.

Overspeed training is designed to improve your stride rate (number of steps per second) and stride length. Overspeed training should be scheduled second in the workout, immediately following your stretching exercises and general warm-up. Overspeed training forces you to take faster and longer steps than you are capable of taking on your own. It therefore requires the complete absence of fatigue.

Scrimmage should be third and follows overspeed training. Remember that the body is still unfatigued, less apt to be injured, and more likely to execute skills at high speed under game conditions.

Drills for the purpose of skill development, if applicable and needed on a particular day, are fourth, while you are still relatively free from fatigue and can execute at high speed under game conditions.

Calisthenics are used to improve general conditioning, develop strength and muscular endurance, and improve aerobic fitness. They are conditioning oriented and should not be in the beginning of your workout. Thirty minutes of hard calisthenics will only change a fresh athlete into a fatigued one. Such fatigue will interfere with your skill and timing and make you more susceptible to injury. Conditioning calisthenics should be either the last or the next-to-last part of the workout.

Wind sprints (interval sprint training as commonly used in football, baseball, and basketball) are also a conditioning activity designed to improve your speed endurance. Such training should be near the end of the workout rather than in the beginning.

Strength/power training (weight training, plyometrics, or sprint loading) is the most fatiguing of any program. It leaves you weak and vulnerable to injury. It is therefore placed as the very last item in your workout.

Sound complicated? It really is not. Continue reading and you will see exactly how the order of activities is used during your preseason period, when you are fully concentrating on speed improvement, and the in-season maintenance period, when you are trying to maintain the improvements you have made.

Preseason Speed Improvement Training

The final order for your preseason speed improvement program is listed in Table 4.1. Follow this order carefully during the preseason. Strength training (weights) and plyometrics are alternated every other day. Overspeed training is used only 3 times per week.

Sample 8-week preseason programs are shown in Tables 4.2, 4.3, and 4.4 for football, basketball, and baseball, respectively. For best results, count back 16 weeks from the start of your in-season period. You should start your preseason efforts no later than that date. Begin with Steps 1, 2, 3, and 4 of the 7-Step Model for 4 to 8 weeks, using the final 8-week period to concentrate on Steps 5, 6, and 7,

Table 4.1 Order of Use for Training Programs in Each Workout

Training program	Length (min)	Workout order	Frequency	Explanation
Stretching and general warm-up	8–12	1	Daily	End your warm-up session with 2 to 4 repetitions of 25-yd walk-jog-stride-sprint cycles.
Sprint-assisted (overspeed training)	30	2	2–3 per week	You should be completely free from fatigue before using any overspeed program.
Form training	15–20	3	Twice per week	Practice both the start and sprinting form.
Speed endurance training	20	4	2–3 per week	Your main objective is to develop explosive power and exhaust the anaerobic system using a combination of short and long distance pickup sprints.
Strength/power training	30–40	5	Every other day	This is the last program in your workout because it produces extreme fatigue.
Plyometrics	15–20	6	1–2 per week	This is always the last program in your workout; should not be used on days that you engage in weight training
Warm-down	8–12	7	Daily	Light jogging and stretching

Table 4.2 Sample Preseason Speed Improvement Program for Football Players

Phase	Week	Training programs	Length (min)	Progression
D-day: Competition begins	0	Football practice begins		
	1-2 prior	Super-refueling program.		These 2 weeks are necessary to allow your body to gain all the refueling benefits from your hard work to this point. Reduce the amount of work you do. Continue to include a few high-intensity workouts (speed and strength) to keep your high-quality edge. You want to begin your football season with enthusiasm; therefore, load your tanks both mentally and physically with rest and high-energy nutrition (see chapter 5).
Preparatory: 4th-quarter development	3-8	Form training	25	Practice your start for 8-10 min each workout along with the speed-form drills devised by Ralph Mann (chapter 3, Step 6). Have your coach reevaluate your form in both the start and the sprinting action.
		Overspeed training	30	Continue with the progression described in the overspeed program in chapter 3, Step 7. Work up to the highest number of repetitions. Begin the advanced program. Think turnover; shorten strides slightly.
		Football skill session	45	Integrate your newly found speed and quickness into football skills.

Day	Activity		Description
Mon./Wed.	Weight training	60 or more	Continue with the recommended methods given in chapter 3, Steps 1 and 2 of the 7-Step Model. Be certain to explode through each repetition.
Wed. at breakpoint	Sprint loading		Hill bursts (2.5- to 8-degree stadium steps or hill) for 10–60 yd using 4–6 repetitions; 10-sec bursts. Follow the recommendations given in chapter 3, Step 5 of the 7-Step Model.
Tues./Thurs.	Form training in the start and sprinting	25	Speed-form drills devised by Ralph Mann.
	Football skill session Sporting speed		Integrate speed into your football drills. (Tues.) High-speed sprinting is the major objective; think speed and quickness as you work out; apply the methods described in Step 6 of the 7-Step Model.
			(Thurs.) Speed endurance is the major objective; use repeated high-speed sprints following the program described in Step 6 of the 7-Step Model. Use some backward high-speed sprints on both a level and a slightly inclined surface to develop the hamstring muscle group.
	Sprint loading		Follow the program described in Step 5 of the 7-Step Model.

(Cont.)

Table 4.2 (Cont.)

Phase	Week	Training programs	Length (min)	Progression
		Plyometrics	10–15	Continue the program described in Step 4 of the 7-Step Model.
		Aerobics	15–30	(Thurs.) 15–30 min of continuous work at your target heart rate.
Fri.		Football skill session		Integrate speed into your football drills.
		Muscle endurance		Circuit training; 3 sets at 50%–85% RM, 8–12 repetitions, resting 15–40 sec between exercises.
		Aerobics	15–30	15–30 min of continuous work at your target heart rate.
Sat.		Body control	160	Games, martial arts.
Sun.		Rest		

Note. Each workout begins with a warm-up period consisting of careful flexibility exercises and walk-jog-stride-sprint cycles and ends with a cool-down period. Retest yourself in the five areas at the end of 2 and 3 months of training.

Table 4.3   Sample Preseason Speed Improvement Program for Baseball Players

Phase	Week	Training programs	Length (min)	Progression
D-day: Competition begins	0	Baseball practice begins		
	1-2 prior	Super-refueling program.		These 2 weeks are necessary to allow your body to gain all the refueling benefits from your hard work to this point. Reduce the amount of work you do. Continue to include a few high-intensity workouts (speed and strength) to keep your high-quality edge. You want to begin your baseball season with enthusiasm; therefore load your tanks both mentally and physically with rest and high-energy nutrition (see chapter 5).
Preparatory: 4th-quarter development	3-8 prior	Form training	25	Practice your start for 8-10 min each workout along with the speed-form drills devised by Ralph Mann (chapter 3, Step 6). Work on the crossover step, breaking right and left, and over shoulder sprinting. Have your coach re-evaluate your form in both the start and the sprinting action.
		Overspeed training	30	Continue with the progression described in the overspeed program in chapter 3, Step 7. Work up to the highest number of repetitions. Begin the advanced program. Think turnover; shorten strides slightly.
		Baseball skill session	45	Integrate your newly found speed and quickness into baseball skills.

(Cont.)

Table 4.3 (Cont.)

Phase	Week	Training programs	Length (min)	Progression
Mon./Wed.		Weight training	60 or more	Continue with the recommended methods given in chapter 3, Steps 1 and 2 of the 7-Step Model. Be certain to explode through each repetition.
Wed. at breakpoint		Sprint loading	25	Hill bursts (2.5- to 8-degree stadium steps or hill) for 10–60 yd using 4–6 repetitions; 10-sec bursts. Follow the recommendations given in chapter 3, Step 5 of the 7-Step Model.
Tues./Thurs.		Form training in the start and sprinting	25	Speed-form drills devised by Ralph Mann.
		Baseball skill session		Integrate speed into your baseball drills.
		Sporting speed	30	(Tues.) High-speed sprinting is the major objective; think speed and quickness as you work out; apply the methods described in Step 6 of the 7-Step Model.
				(Thurs.) Speed endurance is the major objective; use repeated high speed sprints following the program described in Step 6 of the 7-Step Model.

Day	Activity	Min	Description
	Sprint loading	30	Use some backward high-speed sprints on both a level and a slightly inclined surface to develop the hamstring muscle group.
	Plyometrics	10–15	Follow the program described in Step 5 of the 7-Step Model.
	Aerobics	15–30	Continue the program described in Step 4 of the 7-Step Model. (Thurs.) 15–30 min of continuous work at your target heart rate.
Fri.	Baseball skill session	30 or more	Integrate speed into your baseball drills.
	Muscle endurance		Circuit training; three sets at 50%–85% RM, 8–12 repetitions, resting 15–40 sec between exercises.
	Aerobics	15–30	15–30 min of continuous work at your target heart rate.
Sat.	Body control	160	Games, martial arts.
Sun.	Rest		

Note. Each workout begins with a warm-up period consisting of careful flexibility exercises and walk-jog-stride-sprint cycles and ends with a cool-down period. Retest yourself in the five areas at the end of 2 and 3 months of training.

Table 4.4 Sample Preseason Speed Improvement Program for Basketball Players

Phase	Week	Training programs	Length (min)	Progression
D-day: Competition begins	0	Basketball practice begins		
	1–2 prior			Super-refueling program. These 2 weeks are necessry to allow your body to gain all the refueling benefits from your hard work to this point. Reduce the amount of work you do. Continue to include a few high-intensity workouts (speed and strength) to keep your high-quality edge. You want to begin your basketball season with enthusiasm; therefore load your tanks both mentally and physically with rest and high-energy nutrition (see chapter 5).
Preparatory: 4th-quarter development	3–8 prior	Form training	25	Practice the speed-form drills devised by Ralph Mann (chapter 3, Step 6). Work on the crossover step, breaking right and left, and over shoulder sprinting. Have your coach reevaluate your form in both the start and the sprinting action.
		Overspeed training	30	Continue with the progression described in the overspeed program in chapter 3, Step 7. Work up to the highest number of repetitions. Begin the advanced program. Think turnover; shorten strides slightly.
		Basketball skill session	45	Integrate your newly found speed and quickness into basketball skills.

Mon./Wed.	Weight training	60 or more	Continue with the recommended methods given in chapter 3, Steps 1 and 2 of the 7-Step Model. Be certain to explode through each repetition.
Wed. at breakpoint	Sprint loading	25	Hill bursts (2.5- to 8-degree stadium steps or hill) for 10–60 yd using 4–6 repetitions; 10-sec bursts. Follow the recommendations given in chapter 3, Step 5 of the 7-Step Model.
Tues./Thurs.	Form training in the start and sprinting	25	Speed-form drills devised by Ralph Mann.
	Basketball skill session		Integrate speed into your basketball drills.
	Sporting speed	30	(Tues.) High-speed sprinting is the major objective; think speed and quickness as you work out; apply the methods described in Step 6 of the 7-Step Model. (Thurs.) Speed endurance is the major objective; use repeated high speed sprints following the program described in Step 6 of the 7-Step Model. Use some backward high-speed sprints on both a level and a slightly inclined surface to develop the hamstring muscle group.

(Cont.)

Table 4.4 (Cont.)

Phase	Week	Training programs	Length (min)	Progression
		Sprint loading	30	Follow the program described in Step 5 of the 7-Step Model.
		Plyometrics	10–15	Continue the program described in Step 4 of the 7-Step Model. Emphasize the vertical leaps and bounds.
		Aerobics	15–30	(Thurs.) 15–30 min of continuous work at your target heart rate.
Fri.		Basketball skill session		Integrate speed into your basketball drills.
		Muscle endurance	30 or more	Circuit training; 3 sets at 50%–85% RM, 8–12 repetitions, resting 15–40 sec between exercises.
		Aerobics	15–30	15–30 min of continuous work at your target heart rate.
Sat.		Body control	160	Games, martial arts.
Sun.		Rest		

Note. Each workout begins with a warm-up period consisting of careful flexibility exercises and walk-jog-stride-sprint cycles and ends with a cool-down period. Retest yourself in the five areas at the end of 2 and 3 months of training.

after you are certain your foundation is again strong. Plan to retest yourself at the end of the second and third months (use your speed profile form in Appendix C to chart your progress). Your coach will test you at the start of the in-season period. Take your program seriously and devote your attention to each phase of the program along with proper nutrition during this critical improvement period. This is the key time for you to focus only on improving your speed in short distances. No other period of time allows you to devote your efforts totally to one objective—getting faster for your sport. Make it pay off.

In-Season Speed Improvement Training

Once your sports season begins, it will be necessary to continue a modified speed improvement routine to maintain the gains you made during the preseason. You will no longer be able to devote your workout solely to speed improvement. Such a routine is needed to prevent the loss of strength, power, flexibility, speed, and quickness. You must follow the maintenance loads shown in Table 4.5 during the in-season period.

Speed Improvement Suggestions for Football, Basketball, and Baseball Coaches During the In-Season Period

The typical practice session during the in-season period does not allow one to develop high levels of strength, power, speed, speed endurance, flexibility, and aerobic fitness. The use of such programs creates two major problems: the order in which these programs should be used in a practice session and how they fit into a tight schedule.

Although time becomes precious during the competitive season in football, basketball, and baseball, it is not difficult to work with the maintenance loads to prevent loss of speed. Only a slight adjustment and departure from the normal practice routine will be necessary. It is recommended that coaches

Table 4.5 Maintenance Loads to Prevent Loss of Speed Improvement Training Effect During the In-Season Period

Quality	In-season maintenance loads
Flexibility	2-3 sessions per week
Speed (improved stride rate and length and improved acceleration and power)	2 half-hour overspeed workouts per week (5-8 towing pulls each session)
Strength/power	1 vigorous weight-training workout per week plus one plyometric session
Muscle bulk	2 weight-training sessions per week
Speed endurance	2 pickup sprint training workouts per week
Sport speed	4-5 practice sessions per week in your specific sport

- commit a small portion of each practice day to speed improvement;
- include at least a minimum amount of testing twice per season in the five key areas described in chapter 2 to locate weaknesses that are restricting fast movement and preventing athletes from reaching their speed potential;
- assign a sprint coach specifically to this task (the track coach is generally an excellent choice);
- eliminate traditional wind sprints from the program and substitute with the pickup-sprint program described in chapter 3;
- eliminate calisthenics from the beginning of each practice session and replace with flexibility stretching exercises followed by overspeed training (use calisthenics at the end of your workout schedule);
- use explosive power/strength training (weight training) and overspeed training 1 to 2 times per week to maintain the strength, power, and speed acquired during the preseason period;
- use plyometric training no more than 1 to 2 times per week (on days when maintenance weight training is not scheduled); and
- use the speed improvement maintenance programs in the proper order.

Exactly how would this work in a scheduled practice session? Table 4.6 answers this question and shows you the minimum times needed for each program and the exact order in which it should take place. As you can see, it can be done with only minor adjustments. A warm-up period of stretching exercises is used at the beginning of the workout, followed by overspeed training when you are free from fatigue. The skill development phase of your sport (scrimmage, drills, etc.) then takes place and is followed by the conditioning phase (pickup sprints, calisthenics, strength training, and plyometrics) and a brief warm-down period.

Speed Week

The Dallas Cowboys use another unique approach, referred to as ''Speed Week'' that they find easy for players to understand and apply and that is very effective. Speed Week divides each 7-day period into 3 phases:

Table 4.6 Practice Placement of Speed Improvement Training Programs During the In-Season Period

Time (min)	Order	Program	Purpose	Comments
6–7	1	Flexibility exercises	Increased range of motion, warm-up effect, and increased stride	Little conditioning value; warm-up prior to vigorous exercise without fatigue
10–18	2	Overspeed training	Increased stride rate and length and improved acceleration	Short session while athletes are free from fatigue
75–120	3	Normal session in football, basketball, baseball	Mastery of skills, strategy, and conditioning	Major portion of practice
15	4	Calisthenics, pickup sprints	General conditioning	Major thrust of conditioning program
15–20	5	Weight training or plyometrics	Power, strength, acceleration	2–3 times per week for improvement, once per week to maintain

Early Nonfatigued Phase (Monday/Tuesday/Wednesday morning).
No leg work (strength/power training or endurance training) is permitted during this period. High-intensity work with overspeed training (tubing, Sprint Master, downhill sprinting) dominates this 3-day period while athletes are relatively free from fatigue. The proper order described previously is still followed. Upper-body strength/power training does take place.

Late Fatigued Phase (Wednesday afternoon/Thursday/Friday).
"Breakpoint" day occurs on Wednesday afternoon. Training now moves to strength/power activities (sprint loading, weight training, plyometrics, aerobics) and speed endurance. Overspeed training is not used during this period. The proper order described previously in this chapter is carefully followed.

Rest Period (Saturday).   Light workout combined with strategy.

Profile
Craig Reynolds: How He Trains

Age: 34   *Team:* Houston Astros
Height: 6 ft 1 in.   *Position:* Shortstop
Weight: 175 lb   *Career Batting Average:* .258
Body Fat: 13.5%

Career Highlights: Recently completed eleventh season in major leagues; selected to both the American and the National League all-star teams; past recipient of Danny Thompson Award for best exemplifying the Christian way of life; appeared in 90% of Houston Astros games over the past 7 years.

Speed Improvement Program
Craig has maintained a structured in-season total fitness program since joining the Astros in 1980. Workouts consist of daily flexibility and speed exercises, plus strength training on alternate days using Nautilus equipment and dumbbells. Nautilus work is limited to 1 set of 12 exercises plus strength training on alternate days using 12 exercises with 80% of maximum weight. Dumbbell exercises are performed daily for the rotator cuff, hands, and forearms. Stretching exercises are performed daily before, during, and after each workout and game. Speed work consists of .25 to .5 miles of interval, hollow, and pickup sprints on a daily basis.

Profile
Nolan Ryan: How He Trains

Age: 40   *Team:* Houston Astros
Height: 6 ft 2 in.   *Position:* Starting pitcher
Weight: 210 lb   *Career Earned Run Average:*
Body Fat: 12.1%   3.13 with average of 9.5
                                   strikeouts per game for 21
                                   years

Career Highlights: Major league all-time strikeout king (4,547); only pitcher in major leagues to throw five no-hit games; led National League in earned run average (3.08) and strikeouts (270, or 11.5/game) in 1987; highest average velocity (91.3 mph) among National League starting pitchers in 1987 at age 40.

Speed Improvement Program

Nolan pitches on a 5-day rotation; he has 4 days of rest between starts. The season consists of 162 games played during a span of approximately 180 days. In a typical year, he will have about 35 starts, pitch 200–250 innings, and throw almost 4,000 pitches. His primary goal is to maintain total fitness throughout the season. Nolan trains with weights 3 times between starts: the day after he pitches, 2 days before, and lightly for warm-up purposes on the day he pitches. Lifting consists of three sets of 10 repetitions on 12 different Nautilus machines as well as bench presses using free weights.

Nolan also engages in dumbbell exercises for the rotator cuff muscles and, flexibility, abdominal, speed and endurance work on a daily basis. Speed work consists of a series of interval, acceleration, hollow, and sustained sprints of 30 to 110 yards in distances for a total distance run of about half a mile per day. Aerobic work consists of a 20-minute workout on a Fitron bicycle ergometer at a metabolic load equivalent to a 15-minute 2-mile run. Workouts taper off as he nears competition with both speed and aerobic work decreased by approximately 50%.

Profile
Derek Harper: How He Trains

Age: 25

Weight: 203 lb

College Team: University of
   Illinois

NBA Team: Dallas Mavericks
   (fifth year)

Position: Guard

Career Highlights: Field percentage—.504, Free throw percentage—.710, Points per game—10.8

Speed Improvement Program

Pass and shoot are the cornerstones of the Dallas Maverick's conditioning program. The key word to unlock the mysteries of their program is PASS:

P: Play in as many gamelike situations (2-on-2, 3-on-3, 4-on-4, 5-on-5) or drills to integrate the demands required to play basketball. Remember that all mental and physical systems are acting together to create a dynamic unity.

A: Anaerobic energy sources provide the fuel for basketball. *A* is a reminder to build anaerobic capacity by playing the game or by doing quickness, sprinting, and agility training in expected and unexpected situations.

S: Speed, quickness, acceleration, and power are the qualities that separate all ability levels. There can be no substitutes for these qualities in selecting and training elite athletes. Consequently, time is given to develop these qualities through sprint loading, sport speed, and overspeed training (Steps 5, 6, and 7 of the 7-Step Model).

S: Stamina, or the ability to sustain high levels of work output for the duration of the game, is a key quality. If all other qualities are equal, the victory goes to those who played at higher levels of work output for the entire game. In other words, those who fatigue the least will play closer to their maximum levels of speed, quickness, acceleration, and power throughout the game.

Key features of Derek Harper's and other Mavericks' programs:

1. Preseason physicals and player evaluations include body composition and fitness measures.
2. Sport-speed training is the foundation of training. All forms of games and drills are used to increase conditioning levels.
3. Sprints for speed development and maintenance.
4. Speed endurance for sustained high-speed running and sprinting: short course 3.5 times the length of the court (94 feet) in 45 seconds, and long course 7 times the length of the court in 90 seconds.
5. Cardioaerobic training, or the development of the cardiorespiratory systems, is accomplished by jogging, cycling, and swimming.

Profile
Randy White: How He Trains

Born: 1-15-53
Height: 6 ft 4 in.
Weight: 260 lb
Body Fat: 15%
College Team: University of Maryland
NFL Team: Dallas Cowboys, 13th year
Position: All-pro defensive tackle, 9 years

40-Yard-Dash Time: 4.80
20-Yard Time: 2.87
Jerk: 350 lb
Clean: 401 lb
Bench Press: 501 lb
Dead Lift: 600 lb
Back Squat: 600 lb
Vertical Jump: 23.0 in.
880-Yard Time: 3:00
1.5-Mile Time: 11:00
Maximum Oxygen Uptake: 45.0

Speed Improvement Program

Follows 7-Step Model developed by Bob Ward and George B. Dintiman.

	Typical in-season schedule	*Typical preseason schedule*
Monday	Postgame recovery; easy jog and weight training	Overspeed/quickness Decline course Sprint Master Martial arts Handball Football starts Weight training Driving machine
Tuesday	Rest day	Football speed Handball Martial arts Football starts
Wednesday	Speed and strength	Overspeed/quickness Decline course Sprint Master Diagnostic Power Trainer Handball Football starts Weight training Driving machine
Thursday	Speed	Speed endurance Handball Aerobics
Friday	Integrated into football practice	Weight training Diagnostic Power Trainer Handball Martial Arts Aerobics
Saturday	Light warm-up	Active recovery Games (light) Light jog/bike
Sunday	Game day	Active rest

Profile
Bill Bates: How He Trains

Born: 6-6-61
Height: 6 ft 1 in.
Weight: 203 lb
Body Fat: 5.4%
College Team: University of
Tennessee
NFL Team: Dallas Cowboys,
fourth year
Position: Special teams all-pro,
strong safety

40-Yard Dash Time:
As a Rookie—4.79;
current—4.56
20-Yard Time: 2.6
Jerk: 305 lb
Clean: 310 lb
Bench Press: 370 lb
Dead Lift: 465 lb
Front Squat: 320 lb
Vertical Jump: 31.5 in.
880-Yard Time: 2:15
1.5-Mile Time: 10:02
Maximum Oxygen Uptake: 53.4

Speed Improvement Program

Follow 7-Step Model developed by Bob Ward and George B.
Dintiman.

	Typical in-season schedule	*Typical preseason schedule*
Monday	Postgame recovery; easy jog and weight training	Overspeed/quickness Decline course Sprint Master Strong safety skills Handball/tennis/ racquetball/basketball Martial arts Weight training
Tuesday	Rest day	Football speed/quickness Strong safety skills Handball/tennis/ racquetball/basketball Martial arts

Wednesday	Speed and strength	Overspeed/quickness
		Strong safety skills
		Handball/tennis/
		  racquetball/basketball
		Martial arts
		Diagnostic Power
		  Trainer
		Weight training

Thursday	Speed	Speed endurance:
		  8–12 × 110 yards in
		  15 seconds
		Handball/tennis/
		  racquetball/basketball
		Aerobics

Friday	Integrated into football
	  practice
		Weight training
		Diagnostic Power
		  Trainer
		Aerobics

Saturday	Light warm-up	Active recovery Games Light jog/bike
Sunday	Game day	Rest

Chapter 5

Sports Nutrition and Speed Training

Tell me what you eat and I will tell you what you are.
—Anthelme Brillat-Savarin

Sound nutrition is a critical part of your speed-training program. Proper fluid and energy management during training and competition are essential to your health and success. Each of the five main classes of nutrients that foods provide—carbohydrate, protein, fat, vitamins, and minerals—has a specific role in satisfying the fundamental needs of your body. Water, the largest single component of the body, is also an essential nutrient.

In a physically well-trained, well-conditioned state, your body becomes more responsive to dietary management. Proper nutritional management forms the groundwork for sound biological work, the chemicals required for your body's many functions, and the basic elements needed for tissue growth and repair. Improper nutrition can impair the stamina, strength, and endurance that you train so rigorously to achieve.

Good nutrition results from continuously practicing sound dietary habits, not just from following a good diet during competition or the few hours before an event. There are four potentially critical nutrition periods:

1. Nutrition maintenance during training
2. Pre-event nutrition
3. Nutritional support during competition or training
4. Postevent or posttraining nutrition

This chapter was written by Keith B. Wheeler, PhD.

In this chapter, optimal nutrition during these critical periods is discussed, as are the nutritional requirements for effective weight-gain, strength-gain, and weight-loss programs.

Nutritional Maintenance During Training

Although no single diet is totally adequate for all athletes, certain fundamental nutrients are common to all well-balanced diets. A nutritionally adequate diet provides the everyday needs for optimal functioning. The contribution of total calories from carbohydrate, protein, and fat in your diet should fall within the following ranges: carbohydrate, 60–65%; protein, 12–15%, and fat, 25–30% of total calories. Table 5.1 describes a basic diet that satisfies these criteria. This particular diet is also balanced in that it contains nutrients from the four major food groups: (1) milk and milk products, (2) meat and other high-protein foods, (3) fruits and vegetables, and (4) cereal and grain foods.

The Importance of Carbohydrate

Carbohydrate is an important source of energy that is used by the muscles. When muscles cannot get enough carbohydrate, they become fatigued. You therefore need to consume enough carbohydrate each day to meet the energy demands of your speed-training program. Carbohydrate is found in the body primarily in two forms: glycogen and glucose. Glycogen is the form that is stored in the muscle and liver, and glucose is the form that circulates in the blood. When you train, the glycogen content of your muscles progressively decreases if carbohydrate is not replaced. Fatigue occurs when the glycogen in active muscles becomes severely depleted.

A high-carbohydrate dietary regimen will enhance endurance performance. Research has shown that a high-carbohydrate diet is associated with both a higher initial muscle glycogen concentration and greater endurance than are high-fat and normal, mixed diets. The chronic fatigue (''staleness'') associated with aggressive training may be partly related to glycogen depletion brought about by the consumption of inadequate amounts of carbohydrate. This

Table 5.1 A Basic Diet

Meal	Approximate calories
Breakfast:	
2 bowls bran flakes	950
2 c milk (2% fat)	
2 pieces toast (butter and jelly)	
2 c orange juice	
Lunch:	
2 1/2 c macaroni and cheese dinner	1,250
1 banana	
1 granola bar	
1 c milk (2% fat)	
Snack:	
1 doughnut (iced-cake)	350
1 c milk (2% fat)	
1 apple	
Dinner:	
6 pancakes (syrup and butter)	1,450
2 eggs	
2 c milk (2% fat)	
1 c orange juice	
1 banana	
1 pudding (4 oz)	
Total	4,000

chronic fatigue can limit your program and, ultimately, your ability to compete at maximum potential.

One way to delay muscle fatigue is by increasing the amount of glycogen stored in your muscles before an event such as a football, baseball, or basketball game. More glycogen will then be available to the muscle for a longer period of time. This is referred to as glycogen or carbohydrate "loading," or "supercompensation." Although carbohydrate loading, when done properly, does increase muscle glycogen stores above normal, it is not recommended for athletes in most sports.

Carbohydrate loading can be useful for athletes preparing for endurance events a few times a year. However, loading can cause some minor pain in muscles that are glycogen loaded, and the dietary restrictions are difficult to follow. In addition, the complete glycogen-loading regime, which includes a high-fat, high-protein diet phase, should be used cautiously because of potential metabolic and nutritional side effects. In light of the problems with these methods of carbohydrate loading, you should know that the muscle glycogen stores can be doubled simply by increasing your dietary carbohydrate intake above normal for 4 or 5 consecutive days. You must eat 500 to 600 grams of carbohydrate per day (60% to 70% of total calories if consuming 3,000 to 4,000 calories per day).

A nutritional concern that is more important than carbohydrate loading is consuming enough carbohydrate on a daily basis. No matter how well trained you are, some muscle glycogen is used as fuel during moderate or high-intensity exercise. If the carbohydrate intake from your diet is not enough to replace the muscle glycogen used during exercise, muscle glycogen levels will drop below normal. Dietary management of your daily carbohydrate intake can minimize this effect. Low carbohydrate diets (40% or less of total calories from carbohydrate) will cause your muscle glycogen levels to decline with repeated daily exercise. On the other hand, a high-carbohydrate diet (70% of total calories from carbohydrate) produces a glycogen rebound with muscle glycogen stores returning to near-normal levels each day. For athletes in heavy training, such as those following our speed improvement program, a high-carbohydrate diet is essential if you are to receive the maximum benefits from your training.

Pre-event Nutrition

The primary purpose of the pre-event meal is to provide energy and water to support the athlete during the upcoming competition. Gastrointestinal complications, such as stomach cramps or nausea, can be prevented or reduced by restricting certain types of food before competition. For example, gas-producing foods, foods with spicy ingredients, foods high in bulk or fat, and alcohol should be restricted, as should milk and milk products. Psychological considerations are also important. For example, if you believe that certain foods will help you win, they should be part of your pregame meal when possible, keeping in mind the previously mentioned restrictions.

New dietary practices should never be started on the day of an important competition. New food items should be introduced into your diet during the training period. In general, the pregame meal should conform to the following guidelines:

- High-carbohydrate content (60% to 70% of total calories)
- Minimal bulk foods to minimize the residue that accumulates in the stomach and intestines
- Low-salt content to avoid excessive water loss through the urine
- Adequate fluids (two to three 8-ounce glasses of water) to assure hydration

You may eat a heavy meal 3 to 4 hours before competition if desired. As an alternative, a light, high-carbohydrate meal may be eaten 2 to 3 hours before competition. Complete liquid diets can serve as effective pregame meals. The multiple competitive advantages of defined, complete liquid nutritional diets are the following:

- Can be consumed 1 to 2 hours before competition because of short gastric emptying time
- Provide nutrients in forms that are digested and absorbed rapidly
- Assure adequate hydration
- Maintain blood glucose levels during exercise
- May help avoid pregame nausea
- Yield low stool residue, keeping transient weight gain to a minimum
- Provide practical alternative to solid foods for athletes in day-long competition, tournaments, and multiple events
- Can be used for nutritional supplementation during training

Meals consisting of liquid nutritional products are emptied relatively rapidly from the stomach; that is, they have a short "gastric emptying time." Thus, they can be eaten closer to the event (1–2 hours pregame) than can meals of solid foods. Liquid nutritional products offer an effective way to assure adequate nutrition and hydration before competition. They provide a rapidly available supply of nutrients and also may help athletes avoid the pregame nausea sometimes associated with solid foods.

Nutritional Support During Competition and Training

The impact that nutritional support will have during competition depends on the type of exercise. Short-term explosive activities such as sprinting will not be limited by nutrition-related factors, assuming that your nutritional status was normal before the event. In contrast, performance in prolonged events such as distance running, basketball, soccer, or lengthy practice and training sessions in any sport can be influenced by the way fluid and carbohydrate intakes are managed during competition. Proper fluid management during training and competition is vital to health and high-level performance. Improper fluid replacement during exercise will impair the physical performance and endurance that you trained long hours to achieve.

A fluid-energy replacement beverage used during exercise should

- provide a rapidly available source of water (the beverage must empty from the stomach as quickly as plain water);
- deliver a significant quantity of easily digested and absorbed carbohydrate;
- provide an appropriate concentration of important minerals and electrolytes; and
- possess "refreshing" taste characteristics.

Any replacement beverage should be consumed (a) cold (40° to 50° F), (b) in relatively small quantities (8 to 10 ounces), and (c) at frequent intervals (every 15 to 20 minutes). Several studies have demonstrated that carbohydrate intake during an endurance event delays the onset of exhaustion. Carbohydrate probably serves as an energy supply for the working muscles, so muscle glycogen stores are not used up as rapidly. Also, the presence of small quantities of carbohydrate in a fluid-replacement drink enhances the absorption of water and electrolytes, which helps meet your water needs.

Water and carbohydrate supplementation has been shown to improve the endurance of long-distance runners. There is every reason to believe that such supplementation can also help delay fatigue and improve endurance in your sport. Keep in mind that failure to replace fluid loss will definitely result in early fatigue and reduced performance. Drinking 8 ounces of water every 15 minutes or consuming 8 or more ounces of a 7% carbohydrate beverage (glucose polymers plus fructose) every 15 minutes has been shown to delay fatigue and improve endurance. The carbohydrate solution is slightly more effective than plain water. Fluids (water or carbohydrate solution) should be consumed before, during, and after exercise.

The specific type of carbohydrate that should be provided during activity has not been determined conclusively. The carbohydrate used in most commercially available sports solutions are simple sugars (glucose and sucrose). Research has found that if too much glucose or sucrose (table sugar) is added to a sports solution, stomach emptying slows markedly. This decreases the rate that water is available to the athlete and thus will increase the risk of dehydration. Glucose polymers are a better carbohydrate source for fluid-replacement beverages. Glucose polymers are larger than simple sugars but smaller than complex starches. Studies have shown that solutions containing approximately 7% glucose polymers empty from the stomach faster than does an equivalent solution of glucose. Another study found that a carbohydrate solution containing glucose polymers and fructose (44 grams per quart and 24 grams per quart, respectively) does not slow stomach emptying time. If glucose polymers rather than free glucose or sucrose are used in a fluid-replacement beverage, more carbohydrate can be delivered without delaying the absorption of water. Figure 5.1

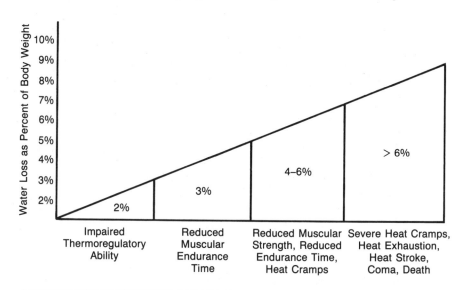

Figure 5.1 Relationship between fluid loss (% of total body weight) and physiological functions.

demonstrates why the availability of water is so critical to performance. Performance will be compromised when water loss approaches 3% of body weight.

Electrolytes

In terms of physical activity, the important minerals in your body are sodium, potassium, chloride, calcium, and magnesium. These minerals may be a part of other compounds in the body or may exist alone in forms that have small electrical charges. Thus, these minerals are often called *electrolytes*. Sodium and chloride are found mainly in the blood, while potassium and magnesium are found mainly within the cells of the body.

A balanced diet is a safe and adequate source of minerals. In general, supplementation with minerals will not enhance your physical performance, particularly because exercise does not appear to cause a significant increase in mineral requirements. Some individuals advocate the use of salt tablets, but in most cases salt tablets compound dehydration by accelerating the loss of water. Even when an athlete is losing 3% to 4% of body weight as water on a daily basis, salt tablets are not necessary and can actually be dangerous.

During some prolonged, intense physical activities such as two-a-day football drills, you may experience daily water losses in excess of 5%–6% of your body weight. An electrolyte deficit can develop with this much fluid loss day after day. Electrolyte replacement should be considered under these conditions; however, it should be consumed in very dilute solutions during physical activity. A good guideline to follow is a maximum of 230 mg (10 mEq) sodium, 355 mg (10 mEq) chloride, and 195 mg (5 mEq) potassium per quart of solution. These concentrations are adequate to correct any potential deficit but are not high enough to slow the gastric emptying of the sports solution.

Postevent Nutrition

Once competition has ended for the day, the nutritional management used during training again becomes appropriate. Because you must recover from the stress of competition and return to normal training as soon as possible, the body's fluid and energy reserves must be restored rapidly. You can increase the rate of recovery by consuming a high-carbohydrate meal as soon as possible following competition or a workout. The rate of glycogen synthesis in the muscle has been demonstrated to be twice as rapid when carbohydrate is consumed within the first 10 minutes following exercise compared with waiting 2 hours.

In most individuals, appetite is supressed following exhaustive exercise. It may be difficult for you to consume a solid-food meal that is high in carbohydrate immediately following competition or an intense training period. During this period of time, a concentrated liquid carbohydrate supplement can be useful in delivering the necessary carbohydrate calories when they are most needed. You should try to consume at least 1.5 grams of carbohydrate per kilogram of body weight within 2 hours after exhaustive exercise (i.e., 136 grams of carbohydrate for a 200-pound athlete).

Weight Control

In most sports, weight management and energy production go together. Because the energy requirements of many sports are so high, athletes must eat to gain energy despite the fact that most of the calories consumed are burned. As a result, some individuals have difficulty consuming enough calories to support an intensive training program. These individuals usually cannot maintain a desired body weight throughout a competitive season and may actually lack the muscle mass (strength) to compete successfully. These players may need to add extra weight in the form of muscle.

Other players may be carrying extra weight in the form of body fat, thus compromising their speed and agility. For these individuals, the challenge is to lose fat weight without losing or diminishing muscle mass.

Gaining Lean Body Weight

One pound of muscle is equivalent to approximately 3,500 calories; therefore, if you want to gain a pound of muscle mass during a period of time, you must exceed normal caloric requirements by that amount. Also, the extra calories must be supported by an appropriate exercise regimen, or the weight gain will be deposited primarily as fat, not lean body mass. A weight gain of more than 1 to

1.5 pounds per week should not be attempted. Athletes should avoid consuming more than 1,000 calories per day in excess of the normal required intake as excessive calories will promote fat deposition.

The excess calories should contain moderate levels of protein (12% to 15% of total calories) with the remainder mainly deriving from carbohydrates and some fat. These calories, along with your training program, will ensure that the protein you consume is efficiently used for new tissue development. A common problem among athletes who wish to gain muscle mass is their inability to consume the appropriate amount of calories during an aggressive training program. Nutritionally complete liquid supplements that are high in carbohydrate can be used to help satisfy daily nutrient requirements.

Some individuals mistakenly believe that high protein intakes (i.e., protein powders, amino acid tablets or liquid protein supplements) are necessary to achieve increases in muscle mass and strength. However, high protein intakes have never been shown to be uniquely beneficial to athletes. If consumed in excess of requirement, protein is used as an energy source. Protein is not stored in the body per se. If it is not needed to make tissue, blood components, or supportive material, it must be degraded and used as energy or converted to fat and stored. Protein synthesis cannot be stimulated simply by increasing protein intake. Controlled research trials have not shown elevated protein intakes to have beneficial effects on strength, power, or muscular endurance.

Eating excessive amounts of protein not only offers no obvious benefit but may actually hamper your performance. The uncontrolled intake of protein (from powders and tablets) can worsen dehydration and cause gastrointestinal disturbances (e.g., diarrhea).

Losing Fat Weight

Properly losing weight takes discipline and patience. The most healthful way to accomplish body-fat loss is to maintain or increase exercise while reducing food intake. Starvation and crash diets are not effective because muscle tissue begins to break down.

For each pound of fat loss desired, 3,500 calories need to be eliminated from the diet. Losing 2 pounds in a week, for example, requires an energy deficit of 7,000 calories, or 1,000 calories per day—a lot of calories to remove from the diet at a time when energy demands are increasing. A more realistic way to lose the 2 pounds is to eat 500 fewer calories each day and to burn an additional 500 calories each day for a week. The rate of loss should not exceed 2 pounds per week. Rates faster than this may be dangerous, especially in young boys and girls.

Dietary intake should not fall below 2,000 calories per day for young boys and 1,700 calories per day for young girls. Fewer calories may compromise growth, especially for those who are involved in a vigorous training program.

Summary

Although it is widely accepted that a poor nutritional state is not compatible with optimal physical performance, athletes do not always follow proper dietary guidelines. Too often, athletes and coaches are influenced by half-truths or misinformation about nutrition. Nutritional practices may be adopted that not only offer no measurable advantages but also, if carried to excess, are potentially dangerous. In contrast, a balanced nutritional regimen provides the athlete with energy and all the basic nutrients needed for tissue growth and replacement.

Nutritional conditioning is a daily concern for the athlete. Nutritional considerations should not be limited to event days but should be applied during your entire speed-training period—the phase of your program in which nutritional management can have its greatest effect.

Suggested Readings

Find out how much everyone else knows and you'll discover how very much there is still to be learned.
—George B. Dintiman

Abraham, W. M. (1976). Exercise induced muscle soreness. *Sportsmedicine, 7*, 57-60.

American Alliance for Health, Physical Education and Recreation. (1982). *Nutrition for athletes*. Reston, VA: American Alliance for Health, Physical Education and Recreation.

American Medical Association. (1971). *The Wonderful Human Machine*. Chicago: Author.

Anderson, B. (1980). *Stretching*. Bolinas, CA: Shelter Publications.

Åstrand, P.O., & Rodahl, K. (1977). *Textbook of work physiology: Physiological basis of exercise*. New York: McGraw Hill.

Beaulieu, J.E. (1982). *Stretching for all sports*. Pasadena, CA: Athletic Press.

Bergstron, J., & Hultman, E. (1972). Nutrition for maximal sports performance. *Journal of the American Medical Association, 221*, 999.

Bompa, T. (1983). *Theory and methodology of training—The key to athletic performance*. Dubuque, IA: Kendall Hunt.

Brody, D.M. (1980). Running injuries. *Clinical Symposia, 32*(4), 36.

Broom, E. (1962). Sprint questions and answers. *Track Technique, 10*, 302-305.

Cantu, R.C. (1983). *Sports medicine in primary care*. Lexington, MA: The Collamore Press, D.C. Heath.

Cantu, R.C. (1983). *Sports medicine, sports science: Bridging the gap*. Lexington, MA: The Collamore Press, D.C. Heath.

Cooper, K.H. (1982). *The aerobics program for total well-being*. New York: M. Evans.

Croce, P. (1983). *Stretching for athletics*. West Point, NY: Leisure Press.

Darden, P. (1983). *Especially for women*. West Point, NY: Leisure Press.

Dintiman, G. (1964). The effects of various training programs on running speed. *Research Quarterly, 35*, 456-463.

Dintiman, G. (1966). The relationship between the ratio, leg strength/body weight and running speed. *The Bulletin of the Connecticut Association for Health, Physical Education and Recreation, 11*, 5.

Dintiman, G. (1970). *Sprinting speed: Its improvement for major sports competition*. Springfield, IL: Charles C Thomas.

Dintiman, G. (1974). *What research tells the coach about sprinting*. Reston, VA: American Alliance for Health, Physical Education and Recreation.

Dintiman, G. (1979). *How to run faster: A do-it-yourself book for athletes in all sports*. Richmond, VA: Champion Athlete.

Dintiman, G. (1984). *How to run faster: Step-by-step instructions on how to increase foot speed*. Champaign, IL: Human Kinetics.

Dintiman, G. (1985, August). Sports speed. *Sports Fitness Magazine*, pp. 70-73, 92.

Dintiman, G. (1987, April). A faster athlete is a better athlete. *Sport-speed Magazine*, pp. 3-5.

Dintiman, G., Coleman, G., & Ward, B. (1985, May). Speed improvement for baseball. *Sports Fitness Magazine*, pp. 118-119.

Dintiman, G., Davis, R., Pennington, J., & Stone, S. (1984). *Discovering lifetime fitness*. Minneapolis: West.

Dintiman, G., & Greenberg, J. (1984). *Health through discovery* (4th edition). New York: Random House.

Dintiman, G., & Stone, S. (1983). *A parent's guide to weight control for children*. Richmond, VA: Champion Athlete.

Dintiman, G., & Unitas, J. (1979). *Improving health and performance in the athlete*. Englewood Cliffs, NJ: Prentice-Hall.

Dintiman, G., & Unitas, J. (1982). *The athlete's handbook: How to be a champion in any sport*. Englewood Cliffs, NJ: Prentice-Hall.

Dintiman, G., & Ward, B. (1988). *Train America: Achieving peak performance and fitness*. Dubuque, IA: Hendor/Hunt.

Falls, H., Baylor, A., & Dishman, R. (1980). *Essentials of fitness*. Philadelphia: W.B. Saunders.

Gowitzkie, B., & Milner, M. (1980). *Understanding the scientific basis of human movement*. Baltimore, MD: Williams and Wilkins.

Hales, D., & Hales, R. (1983, July-August). How much is enough. *American Health Magazine*, pp. 120-125.

Hamilton, E., & Whitney, E. (1982). *Nutrition: Concepts and controversies.* Minneapolis: West.

Hardinge, G. (1972). *Water, water, water.* Loma Linda, CA: Loma Linda University School of Health.

Hilsendaager, D., Strow, M., & Acklerman, K. (1969). Comparison of speed, strength, and agility exercises in the development of agility. *Research Quarterly, 40,* 71-75.

Hui, Y. (1985). *Principles and issues in nutrition.* Monterey, CA: Wadsworth.

Jarrell, S. (1982). *Workout with weights.* New York: Arco.

Jordan, J. (1969). Physiological and anthropometrical comparisons of negroes and whites. *Journal of Health, Physical Education, and Recreation, 40,* 93-99.

Katch, F., & McArdle, W. (1983). *Nutrition, weight control and exercise.* Philadelphia: Lea & Febiger.

Klafs, C., & Arnhein, D. (1981). *Modern principles of athletic training* (5th Ed.). St. Louis: C.V. Mosby.

Marshall, J., & Barbash, H. (1981). *The sports doctors fitness book for women.* New York: Delacorte.

Morris, A. (1984). *Sports medicine: Prevention of athletic injuries.* Dubuque, IA: William C. Brown.

Osman, J. (1978). *Thin from within.* New York: Hart.

Radcliffe, J., & Farentinos, R. (1985). *Plyometrics: Explosive power training.* Champaign, IL: Human Kinetics.

Riley, D., & Peterson, J. (1979). *Not for men only: Strength training for women.* Champaign, IL: Human Kinetics.

Rosenzweig, S. (1982). *Sports fitness for women.* New York: Harper & Row.

Sandwick, C. (1967). Pacing Machine. *Athletic Journal, 47,* 36-38.

Science and Education Administration, U.S. Department of Agriculture. (1981). *Nutrition and Your Health: Dietary Guidelines for Americans.* Washington, DC: U.S. Government Printing Office.

Smith, N. (1976). *Food for sport.* Palo Alto, CA: Bull.

Stull, A., & Cureton, T. (1980). *Encyclopedia of physical education, fitness and sports: Training, environment, nutrition and fitness.* Salt Lake City: Brighton.

Torg, J. (1983). *Foot and ankle problems in the athlete.* Philadelphia: W. B. Saunders.

Ward, B., & Dintiman, G. (1985). *Speed and explosion.* 60:00 videocassette.

Ward, B., & Dintiman, G. (1988). *Speed and explosion consultant manual*. Richmond, VA: National Association of Speed and Explosion.

Ward, R. (1987, April). Training models for sport. *Sportspeed Magazine*, pp. 6-9.

Weiner, N. (1948). Cybernetics. *Scientific American*, **179**: 614.

Westcott, W. (1982). *Strength fitness: Physiological principles and techniques*. Boston: Allyn & Bacon.

Williams, M. (1983). *Nutrition for fitness and sports*. Dubuque, IA: Brown.

Wilmore, J. (1982). *Training for sports and activity: The physiological basis of the conditioning process*. (2nd Ed.). Boston: Allyn and Bacon.

Yessis, M. (1987). *Yessis review of Soviet physical education/sport*. Fullerton, CA: Author.

Questions and Answers on Speed Improvement

> *Dost thou love life? Then do not squander Time: for that's the stuff Life is made of.*
> *—Benjamin Franklin*

The following are questions that we are frequently asked concerning speed improvement. For your convenience, we have divided them into general and specific categories.

General

Can I become a champion athlete, or are champions born and not made?

Champions are products of hard work, not of heredity. You do not have to be 7 feet tall and weigh 250 pounds to become a champion athlete; nor do you need to be born with superior skill. Keep in mind that *heredity deals the cards, but environment plays the hand.* Some athletes who are born with superior coordination and physical qualities never reach stardom, whereas others with only average qualities become champions. The secret is strong dedication to two areas: skill development for every aspect of your sport and physical development through numerous training programs to allow your body to perform each skill with maximum power, strength, agility, endurance, and speed.

Coordination (skill in hand/eye or foot/eye movements, aerial movements, or any body movements) is specific to the activity, and high levels can be acquired with persistent, correct practice. You have to watch the superstars only once to realize that not all modern-day champions are good all-around athletes. Although there are exceptions, others may be poorly skilled in areas outside their specialty.

Often, the good, young athlete becomes a ''jack-of-all-trades and master of none.'' Some even grow up to be three-sport athletes in college and still never become champions. Many could have become champions had they focused on the one sport most suited for them earlier in their careers.

For most athletes, becoming and remaining a champion requires total dedication to one sport year-round. This is true mainly because the requirements of strength, muscle endurance, power, aerobic endurance, speed, agility, and skill vary from sport to sport. It is not possible to develop these qualities to the level needed to become a champion in more than one or two sports. Muscle bulk, for example, may be helpful in sports such as football, basketball, and baseball but may actually hinder performance in soccer, tennis, or distance running. This is also true of the other qualities. It is wise to begin focusing on your sport by the age of 12 or 13 if you choose an individual sport such as tennis, golf, or running and by the age of 15 or 16 if you choose a team sport such as football, basketball, baseball, soccer, field hockey, rugby, or volleyball.

Once you decide on your best potential sport, go after it with all the reading, training, and practice you can tolerate. Seek the best competition and learn to work on weaknesses until they are strengths. You will not become lightning fast overnight. You need to follow the suggestions in this book for a minimum of 6 months and perhaps for several years if you are a young athlete in your teens. Eventually, your training will pay off.

Modern-day champions are hardworking, dedicated athletes. They did not become champions in 1 year. For many it required at least two workouts every day and countless hours of practicing their skills over a period of 5 to 12 years. Those who eventually made it were the most persistent, dedicated, and hardworking, not necessarily the most genetically blessed.

Can I really improve my speed?

Yes. There is absolutely no reason for doubt. Athletes in almost every sport have improved their times in short distances after following our 7-Step Model for several months. Bill Bates, Dallas

Cowboy special teams expert and free safety, improved his 40-yard time from 4.79 to 4.56 seconds. Carl Bland, split end for the Detroit Lions, went from 4.7 to a 4.5 seconds. One high school athlete improved his time from 5.3 to 4.7 seconds in 6 months. These and other dramatic improvements have been documented in the past several years. Middle and high school athletes who attended our 1-day clinics and 4-day camps have improved as much as .7 seconds. Both Russian and American researchers also have documented improvements in speed when similar programs were used.

What actually makes me sprint faster?

Research shows that you can increase the number of steps taken per second, the length of each step, acceleration time, starting time, and overall speed in short distances. A study of champion and average sprinters found stride lengths to be somewhat similar; the big difference was in stride rate. Champion sprinters took faster steps per second than did average sprinters. Exactly which changes occur at the tissue level is not known. Regardless of the explanation, improvement does occur and you can become faster. It is doubtful that any athlete can reach his or her maximum speed potential without proper speed improvement training. Very few modern-day athletes are sprinting as fast as they are capable of sprinting.

What do fast-twitch and slow-twitch fibers have to do with speed?

There are two basic types of muscle fiber: slow twitch (red) and fast twitch (white). Actually, a third type, fast twitch (red), is grouped with fast twitch (white) for convenience. Slow-twitch (ST) fiber contracts very slowly and is highly fatigue resistant, whereas fast-twitch (FT) fiber fires with more speed and force and is quickly fatigued. Fast-twitch fiber can actually contract up to 3 times faster than ST fiber. For example, the breast muscle of migratory geese is slow-twitch, or red, fiber which enables geese to fly, however slowly, for hours without much fatigue. On the other hand, the breast muscle of the domestic chicken is fast-twitch, or white fiber, enabling it to make its fear-induced short flights through quick, powerful thrusts of the wings. Although the domestic chicken can walk slowly for hours without fatigue (leg muscles are red, or ST, fiber), it can fly for only seconds before fatigue sets in.

It is obvious that being born with a high percentage of FT fiber makes one better suited for sprinting and explosive-type sports such as football, soccer, basketball, and baseball. Some high-caliber sprinters have been found to possess more than 93% FT fiber. Alberto Salazar, one of the best marathon runners of all time, has been found to possess more than 90% ST fiber and is better suited for long, slow activity. Everyone is born with both FT and ST fiber. These fiber types also vary from muscle to muscle. It is possible to find out how much FT and ST fiber you have by performing a muscle biopsy (removing a small amount of tissue from various muscle groups). In our research, we are now experimenting with the standing triple jump to determine its relationship to the percentage of FT fiber in the body. If this test turns out to be a good predictor of the amount of FT fiber in key muscle groups, it will help athletes and coaches devise individual training programs to improve speed.

There is no conclusive evidence to suggest that training will change ST fiber to FT fiber. There are indications that ST fiber and FT (red) fiber begin to take on some of the characteristics of FT (white) fiber with the right kind of training. Perhaps the most important thing to remember is that you are not doomed to slow movement regardless of your muscle makeup. The techniques described in this book have been shown to improve stride length, stride rate, acceleration, and speed in short distances.

Why is ST fiber red and FT fiber white?

A rich supply of blood reaches the ST fiber and produces the red color; a poor supply to FT, or white, fiber results in a pale color.

Why does ST fiber fatigue rapidly and FT fiber slowly?

A poor blood supply to FT fiber results in rapid fatigue that permits only short bouts of all-out anaerobic effort. A rich blood supply to ST fiber allows the removal of fatigue products and the constant use of oxygen (aerobic).

Do certain types of training specifically train different fiber types?

Yes. Research now suggests that explosive-type training (fast muscular contractions in weight training, plyometrics, ballistics, short 15 to 40 yard sprints, overspeed training) increases the thickness and contractual speed of FT fiber. Fast-twitch fiber is recruited during this type of exercise; during lower-intensity exercise, ST fiber is recruited. It is necessary to train explosively to improve your sprinting.

Does heredity limit my potential to be a fast sprinter?

Yes. If you were born with a high percentage of FT fiber, you are more suited for sprinting and explosive movements. Even if you were born with a low percentage of FT fiber, you can still improve your sprinting speed with proper training over a period of 6 months to several years.

Will I get slower with age?

No, unless your conditioning level decreases, you gain weight, or you change your training routine from fast, explosive movements to slow movements.

Is running at maximum speed automatic, or is it necessary to concentrate during a contest?

The mind can concentrate on only one act at a time. The athlete who is thinking about ways to elude a potential tackler or a defensive player in football, about outside problems during a 100-meter dash, or whether the ball is going to be caught while he is running to first base is distracting attention away from the important skill, namely, the act of sprinting as fast as possible. You must concentrate on sprinting and make an effort to accelerate and attain maximum speed. Failure to do so may result in submaximum speed. This explains why a fast runner is occasionally caught from behind by a slower player or why upsets occur in sprinting events. Sprinting step for step with a receiver in football, lateral movement at top speed to maintain proper defensive position in guarding the dribbler in basketball, or sprinting for a line drive in baseball all require concentration on that act without distraction from the outside.

Concentration is also important in the "start." Attention is focused on the first muscular movement such as a fast arm action or a quick, high knee lift rather than on the sound of the gun. If attention is focused on the gun, a slower reaction may occur because you then must shift your attention from a sound to your movement. You will hear a 22-caliber pistol sound 6 feet from your head without trying to listen for it.

In every sport there are times when athletes are sprinting at slightly less than 100% their maximum speed. This is often interpreted as loafing when it may be only a lack of concentration. You can prove this to yourself. Time a 40-yard dash while you think about a history exam, your arm movement, or the length of your stride. Compare your time to one you achieved while concentrating only on moving your legs and arms at maximum speed. Sprinting cannot be combined with creative thinking.

What is the proper way to breathe when I sprint?

Through your mouth. This allows air to enter and exit much faster because there is less resistance to overcome. At rest, the most efficient way to breathe is through the nose, which warms, moistens, and cleanses air of foreign particles. However, on hot days air does not need to be warmed, so mouth breathing actually helps to cool the body. During exercise, nose breathing cannot keep up with the high demand for oxygen. To demonstrate this, you need to run a distance of only .25 miles or more with your mouth shut.

Remember that sprinting is a speed endurance activity; that is, it is performed without the need for atmospheric oxygen. If two test scores in the 40-yard dash were compared—one when you held your breath during the entire sprint and the other when you breathed naturally through your nose and mouth—there would be no difference between the two scores. Sprinters have been known to hold their breaths for the entire racing distance of 100 meters without any effect on their times. The reason is that such a short race does not allow enough time for air breathed in from the atmosphere to be used at the tissue level. During a workout, however, you must breathe through both your nose and your mouth to supply enough oxygen to working muscles.

Breathing is a very simple process that involves three steps: (a) gas exchange in the lungs, (b) gas transport to tissue by the blood, and (c) gas exchange between the blood and tissue. The rate of breathing is controlled by the amount of carbon dioxide in the blood rather than by the lack of oxygen. The normal breathing rate varies from 12 to 20 breaths per minute during rest to as high as 50 to 60 during exercise. As conditioning levels improve, breathing rates per minute are lowered.

In general, you will be more efficient if you leave breathing to nature. At rest, each person has a rate and depth of breathing that is most efficient for him or her; nature will find it. In sprinting and swimming, experts disagree as to how to breathe. Forced breathing prior to the command ''Get set'' and then holding the breath until the gun sounds is common. This procedure is thought to improve steadiness and starting quickness. Exercise is one of the few times that it does not pay to keep your mouth shut!

Improving Starting and Acceleration

How can I improve my acceleration time?

All the programs described in the 7-Step Model will help your acceleration time, which depends on the four basic components that determine starting and acceleration speed:

- *Reaction time (RT)* can be significantly improved in the sprint start.
- *Speed of arm-leg movement* can be significantly improved through sprint training, overspeed training (Step 7), explosive power training, and strength training (Steps 1, 2, 3, and 4).
- *Propulsive force of the legs against the blocks* can be significantly improved through explosive power and strength training (Steps 2, 3, 4, and 5).
- *Starting form and technique* can be improved through periodic practice using the various techniques discussed in this chapter (Step 6).

You should practice high-speed starting when you are not fatigued to simulate competitive conditions and reduce the chances of injury. An adequate warm-up always precedes starting practice with a pistol and should consist of 5 to 8 starts.

How can I improve my stride length?

Increasing your stride length, without reducing the rate of leg movement, is an efficient way to improve speed in short distances. Lloyd Bud Winter, famed track coach of San Jose State College, states, ''The secret of sprinting is to have a long stride that carries you low to the ground.''

The length of your stride depends on several factors:

- Sprinting form
- Leg and ankle strength and power
- Flexibility of the hip and ankle joints
- Length of your legs (which obviously cannot be changed)

Form also affects your stride length. In terms of form, the length of your stride is composed of the sum of three separate distances: the distance from the center of gravity to the toe of the takeoff foot at the instant it leaves the ground (controlled mainly by the length of the legs and the flexibility of the hip joint), the horizontal distance that the center of gravity travels while you are in the air (controlled by the speed, angle, height of release, and air resistance), and the horizontal distance that the toe of the lead foot is forward of the center of gravity at the instant of landing.

These three factors are related to form and appear complicated. Actually, the main concern is to contact the ground with your lead foot about 10 inches ahead of your center of gravity. If the center of gravity is behind the lead foot at ground contact, body weight is also behind you, and there is a slowing effect. Although you can increase your stride length by placing the forward foot ahead of the body's center of gravity (overstriding), you will not improve your 40-yard-dash time. Your task is to locate your ideal stride, then focus on other ways to increase it without changing the center of gravity at ground contact.

Leg and ankle strength/power output is an important factor in increasing stride length. Sprinting is merely a series of controlled leaps from one foot to the other that keep the center of gravity over the lead foot each time it contacts the ground. You improve stride length by pushing off with more force and jumping farther. To improve the force of the push-off you must strengthen the muscles of the lower legs, ankles, and feet through weight training and plyometric training (Steps 1, 2, 3, and 4).

Hip power output is the most important factor in increasing your stride length. Hip extensor tension is the greatest contributor to taking a longer, more explosive stride. To improve the power output of this action, all seven steps are involved, but Steps 5, 6, and 7 will provide the greatest improvement in stride length.

Flexibility may be a factor for some athletes who are unable to "stretch out" while sprinting at maximum speed, which prevents them from taking their ideal stride. The proper use of stretching exercises as a part of your regular warm-up routine will improve your range of motion in both the ankle and the trunk areas. Exercises that are designed to improve the range of motion in the shoulders, hip, and ankle should receive the most attention. These exercises should also follow any type of weight-training program.

Overspeed training will help improve stride length by forcing you to take longer steps than you have ever taken (see Step 7).

How much will a 6-inch increase in stride length improve my time?

Table A.1 shows the importance of lengthening your stride by only 6 inches without affecting the stride rate of 4 steps per second. An increase in stride length of 6 inches improves speed by 2 feet per second. Every second, you are now covering 2 additional feet; in 10 seconds, you are covering 20 additional feet, or nearly 7 yards. Depending on your original time, such a change would reduce your 100-yard-dash time by 0.5 to 0.9 seconds and your 40-yard-dash time by 0.3 to 0.5 seconds. A change in 40-yard-dash time from 5.0 to 4.6 seconds is a very large improvement. Inches do indeed make a difference.

Table A.1 Stride-Length Increase and Its Effect on 40-Yard-Dash Time With a Flying Start

	Stride length	Stride rate	Feet per sec	Approximate 40-yd-dash time
Original speed	6 ft ×	4.0 steps per sec	= 24	5.0 sec
New speed	6 ft 6 in. ×	4.0 steps per sec	= 26	4.6 sec

Is limited body fat important?

Yes. For maximum speed, your body fat should be less than 10 percent of your body weight. Because weight charts are inadequate for athletes (even as an estimate of normal weight), the skinfold method or underwater weighing should be used.

What can I do to improve my stride rate?

Stride rate is the sum of the time for ground contact and time in the air. For champion sprinters, this ratio is 2:1 at the start of the race and 1:1.3 to 1:1.5 at maximum speed later in the race. Stride rate is determined by speed, angle, height of release, and air resistance in flight. Of these, release, or ground reaction, forces seem most important.

Females are about 1 second slower than males in the 100-meter dash due to slower stride rates. Ground reaction forces and power differences are the main cause. Also, children run with faster strides than do adults. As height and leg length increases, stride rate decreases. As the lever gets longer, more power is required to move it at the same rate. Again you can see the importance of strength and power training to improving your stride rate.

In the past, the rate of stride frequency was thought to be an unalterable factor fixed at birth by the nervous and muscular systems' ability to produce a rapid contraction and relaxation within the genetic limitations of FT and ST fiber. There is now evidence to the contrary. Higher stride rates are possible in cycling (5.5 to 7.1 per second) than in sprinting (3.10 to 5.1 per second), downhill sprinting, towing with the Sprint Master and surgical tubing, and treadmill sprinting. Overspeed-training methods have significantly increased stride rate in experimental subjects in a number of studies. The limiting factors are external (wind and surface conditions) and internal forces (strength/power ratio, muscle resistance, fat deposits, neurological muscular patterns, and the preponderance of either FT or ST fiber in the involved muscles).

To improve stride rate, then, you must concentrate on overspeed-training methods to alter neurological patterns and strength/quickness/power training to improve the load/power ratio. Improving this ratio is critical to taking faster steps; for female athletes it may be the most important factor as it serves to improve ground reaction forces and lessen the time for ground contact without loss of push-off power.

Should I be getting a "second wind" when I work out?

It depends on the type of training you are doing. In some athletes, breathlessness, rapid pulse, and sore muscles are suddenly relieved. The load that appeared strenuous and may have caused breathlessness subsides. When and if this occurs, an athlete is capable of additional effort. This so-called second wind may not take place for you, or it may happen following some types of exercise but not others. In fact, some athletes complain that they never experience a second wind.

It is not fully understood why second wind occurs or what brings it about. Here are some things that are known:

- It occurs earlier during vigorous exercise than during moderate exercise.
- It is more likely to take place when the weather is hot, when the wind is not chilling, and when you are wearing warm clothing.
- It may come about sooner when a long, vigorous warm-up is used.

Experiment in your training by using a long warm-up, warm clothing, sweat box, or even artificial heat prior to exercise. When you find the technique that brings about sudden relief from physical stress in your sport, use it before competition. Also, warm up properly. For most people, a second wind is really the first, as they quit much too soon to ever have a second one.

What causes muscle soreness following my speed improvement workout?

You may experience one or two types of soreness: (a) general soreness that is present immediately and disappears 3 to 4 hours after your workout or (b) localized soreness that appears 8 to 24 hours after exercising and that persists for several days. The older you are, the longer the period between exercise and the onset of muscle soreness. At age 20, it may appear within a few hours after exercise, at age 25 the following day, and for the 50-year-old not for 2 to 3 days.

The exact cause of muscle soreness is unknown. Regardless of the cause, it hurts, it will impair your performance, and it is almost certain to occur if you report to the first practice in any sport in poor physical condition.

You can reduce the risk of soreness by warming up properly, avoiding bouncing-type stretching exercises, and slowly increasing your exercise effort rather than overextending yourself early in a workout or training program. You also can expect some muscle soreness the day after your first overspeed-training session even if you are in excellent physical condition and have been sprinting in your workout. Overspeed training taxes muscle groups beyond that of normal training techniques such as unaided sprinting.

Is there anything I can do to improve my cutting and faking skill in football and basketball without losing speed?

Yes. This is another neglected area that receives very little attention in athletics. First, let us examine the purpose of a fake. In order of importance, a fake serves to

- neutralize the defender by slowing his movement, breaking his concentration, altering his center of gravity, delaying his total commitment, and placing doubt in his mind;
- change the direction of movement of the defender away from your intended move; and
- draw the defender closer to you so that a cut is effective (cutting must occur 2 to 3 yards from the defender; therefore a fake "straight-ahead" break will draw him within proper distance).

Keep in mind that you fake, first, to neutralize and, second, to go by untouched. Any fake will help neutralize, and any fake is better than no fake at all.

You must practice all types of head, shoulder, and leg fakes daily to develop the proper skill. These basic cuts must also be mastered:

- *Single cut.* Angle away from the defender to force his commitment before planting the outside foot and cutting in the opposite direction.
- *Double cut.* Run at the opponent before planting the left foot and breaking right, only to plant that foot also and return left to go by the defender. The first cut will neutralize, the second will draw, and the third he will be able only to watch.

- *Triple cut (sideline maneuver)*. Plant the left foot and break right, immediately plant the right foot again and break left, and complete the move by planting the left foot and breaking right at full speed.
- *Spins*. For the football player, once contact has been made with a defender, a quick spin to the outside will help prevent the tackler from wrapping his arms around you and prevent his teammates from executing a hard hit on a stationary target—your body. Keep moving, spin, and spin again when contact is made.
- *Collision*. In the open field, lower your head to convince a defender in a one-on-one situation that you will run over him; use one of the fakes described previously when you are 2 to 3 yards away.
- *Dumb runner*. In the open field, break to the outside early (10 yards before reaching the defender). When the defender goes into a sprint, "bow" back early again to convince him you are untricky, but then revert to your original path at full speed when he commits in the other direction. The entire fake resembles the shape of a banana.

Excellent faking skills in football not only improve yardage but also reduce the risk of injury from a hard tackle from any angle. The inability of a defender to "zero in" on Tony Dorsett or Walter Payton is the secret to their longevity as running backs in the National Football League.

Speed Improvement Training and Young Children

When does the growth spurt take place?

Two growth spurts generally occur: the mid-growth spurt and the adolescent growth spurt. The mid-growth spurt occurs at about 5 to 7 years of age for boys and girls; the adolescent growth spurt begins around 11 to 13 years for girls and at 13 to 15 years for boys.

Females grow faster during their adolescent spurt with the pelvic width continuing to expand after growth has ceased. Males have approximately 2 more years than females have to grow before the adolescent growth spurt, which extends growing time and allows the legs to become longer. There are exceptions in both sexes that fall outside these ranges.

Is it harmful for young children under 10 to engage in vigorous exercise?

There is little evidence to indicate that vigorous training has any harmful effect on the body. This is not to imply that the potential for harm is not present. Under competent leadership, almost any sports activity is relatively safe for young athletes, but hazards are present in any sport or activity without such leadership. Much also depends on the sport, the child's emotional makeup, parental expectations, the growth stage of each child, and the basic philosophy of the league.

Consider these factors before deciding on a specific sport or program:

- Full-contact boxing is an inappropriate sport for children under 10 years of age.
- The hazards of collision sports (football, rugby, and lacrosse) are associated with the leadership and the conditions under which a sport is administered more than with the sport itself. Collision sports can be conducted for youngsters with limited risk.
- Marathon running for young children is a questionable activity as it imposes considerable stress on joints during training as well as excessive energy requirements at a time when surplus calories are needed for growth and development.
- A thorough physical examination is necessary prior to any type of participation.
- Leagues or sports that group athletes not only by age but by body size, sex, skill, and maturation are safe choices for young children.
- Children should undergo a good physical preconditioning program before starting the new activity.

There is no sport in existence that requires a child to begin organized, competitive play during the 6- to 10-year age range. A 6- to 10-year-old does not need all-star games, playoffs, high pressure from the public, paid admissions, and other commercialization.

There is no evidence that exposure to these aspects of adult athletics at an early age has any carryover to later athletic performance.

Children should be protected from emotional and physical damage by avoiding high pressure, win-at-all-cost programs. A child's self-concept is far more important than a victory. Look into your local YMCA age group programs if you want a rational, fun approach to sports. Work on basic motor skills such as running, jumping, throwing, and catching, which do carry over to most sports. Children should be encouraged to compete against their own standards and feel good about themselves at any level of competition.

Is speed improvement training harmful to young children?

No, providing some programs in the 7-Step Model are altered. Young children should not engage in heavy weight training or vigorous plyometric training before puberty. On the other hand, strength/power training, using light weights and high repetitions, are helpful as well as safe. Plyometric training should be avoided altogether for this age group. Overspeed training using surgical tubing or downhill sprinting with fewer repetitions will not harm prepubescent children. During the adolescent growth period and thereafter, the model should be used as described in this book.

Is weight training harmful to children?

The ideal time to begin vigorous weight training appears to be during late adolescence, after the growth spurt and the widening of the shoulder girdle. A properly devised program at this time aids recovery time from injuries, helps prevent injuries to the major joints (knee, shoulder, ankle, and neck), provides needed recognition, and allows youngsters to carry out athletic activities more successfully.

Elementary school children (ages 6 to 12) are extremely weak in the upper body. A modified weight-training program beginning at age 8 or 9 may eliminate the need for intense programs in later years and actually allow more rapid development in physical education and athletic skills that require above-average strength. To achieve success in most sports, weight training must be a part of your program. Age group swimmers continue to utilize weight training several times weekly as a part of their regular training routine. No other program is as effective as this one in developing strength. For the elementary school child, however, some pitfalls must be recognized:

1. Heavy weights can overstress the knee joint at a time when ligament strength is weak.
2. Shoulder and elbow joints are experiencing rapid changes and should not be subjected to heavy weights.
3. Injuries due to faulty lifting form and careless use of equipment may occur.

A modified program for young children should be prepared on an individual basis. In general, it should involve total body development (rather than concentrating on one or two areas), light weight (no more than 60% of maximum for any one exercise), and a high number of repetitions (8–20). Elementary school age is a time for developing general coordination through creative, active games. With competent instruction, strength development can be a valuable activity.

The Adolescent Years

Should restrictions be placed on the adolescent?

Yes. A number of injuries, such as stress fractures, are now appearing in the medical literature for children and adolescents. These types of injuries were practically nonexistent prior to the onset of organized sports for youngsters. "Overuse" injuries are quite rare when children and adolescents are left to play by themselves. In competitive sports, however, overuse injuries to soft tissue are common. It is also believed that injuries such as repetitive microtrauma in childhood may be the cause of the near-epidemic proportions of chondromalacia patellae in adults.

Unfortunately, adolescent medicine falls between the internist and the pediatrician, and often neither is interested or knowledgeable about the type of injuries and their treatment and prevention for this age group. The absence of qualified athletic trainers in high schools and a scarcity of sports medicine physicians adds to the problem. If the current trend toward orthopedic surgeons' providing free clinics and tying in with athletic teams continues, the problem could be alleviated.

Is the adolescent period the most important time to exercise?

Yes. This is a critical period for regular exercise for a number of reasons: (a) Hormonal changes occur that promote great increases in cardiovascular fitness and strength with regular exercise. (b) Body fat is gained and the number of fat cells increases and can be reduced with regular exercise. (c) Exercise habits are formed that are likely to be carried over into the adult years. (d) The social age of the adolescent years make sports important to adjustment and proper self-concept. Some private schools require participation in one varsity and one intramural sport per year. This would be an excellent requirement for public secondary schools.

Is the knee more likely to be injured during the growth years?

Yes. In fact, a hard blow to the knee can produce very serious injuries at certain ages.

High school athletes are more susceptible to injury than are college athletes. The following general traits are present at various age levels:

- *8 years.* General looseness of collateral and anterior cruciate ligaments; high degree of bilateral knee hyperextension
- *8 to 13 years.* Tightening of collateral ligaments and reduction of bilateral hyperextension (great flexibility in cruciates remains); general looseness of knee
- *14 to 16 years.* Still greater looseness evident in the right medial, left medial, and left lateral ligaments; bilateral hyperextension increased; hyperextension increased; bilateral looseness of the anterior cruciates decreased
- *16 to college years.* General tightening of ligament tension and total joint structure
- *College age and older.* General leveling off, with ligament tension remaining fairly constant

It is obvious that the knee is not fully developed for contact sports until about age 16. The exact age differs for each athlete, depending on his or her physiological development. Before this time, contact sports can be dangerous. For example, a hard blow from the side when the foot is planted could cause a serious injury.

Injury Prevention and Your Speed Improvement Program

Injuries can cause you to lose valuable speed-training time. Many injuries can be prevented. You also can reduce the chances of experiencing certain types of injuries common to your sport by following the tips discussed below.

What can I do to reduce my risk of injury in sports?

Follow the 9-point injury prevention program below:

1. *Improve your general conditioning level.* The first step in injury proofing your body is to attain a high degree of general conditioning. It is important to be extra careful in the first several months of a newly begun exercise program (such as speed improvement training), when you are especially vulnerable to muscle, ligament, and joint injuries. All types of injury are also more likely to occur when you are in a state of general fatigue, which causes a reduced blood supply to muscles. Fibers are weakened and easily torn, and joint stability and muscle groups are weakened. This state of general fatigue is common during the early stages of an exercise program. It is also helpful to strengthen the injury-prone areas such as the ankle, wrist, knee, shoulders, lower back, and neck before beginning a new sport.

2. *Analyze your medical history.* If you have been inactive for more than 6 months, are over 30 years of age, or are in the high-risk group (obesity, high blood pressure, diabetes, high blood lipids), a thorough physical examination is recommended. Your resting heart rate and blood pressure and exercise heart rate and blood pressure will provide some clues to your body's response to the new exercise program. Although the chances of a serious problem are slight, it is better to be safe than sorry.

3. *Warm up properly.* At the beginning of all speed improvement workouts, it is important to raise body temperature 1 to 2 degrees to prepare muscles, ligaments, and tendons for vigorous movement. A few extra minutes of warm-up can prevent common muscle pulls, strains, sprains, and lower-back discomfort and can reduce muscle soreness 8 to 24 hours later. Muscle temperature will rise for 25 to 30 minutes during exercise and drop rapidly when activity stops. After 40 to 45 minutes of rest, additional warm-up is needed if you plan to exercise again. Warm up for 10 to 20 minutes or until perspiration is present. The two main ingredients of any warm-up routine are proper stretching and formal exercise (light, easy movement in the same activity as your exercise program; jogging before you run; shooting and dribbling before the basketball game; or catching, throwing, sprinting, and hitting before a baseball game).

4. *Use a cool-down period.* Experienced joggers and runners complete the final half mile or so at a slow, easy pace rather than with a "kick." The final 5 to 15 minutes of any workout can also be used to taper off and cool the body slowly to a near-resting state.

5. *Progress slowly.* It takes a minimum of 6–8 weeks for speed improvement work to pay off. You will improve slowly each day, and attempts to perform herculean workouts will not speed up your progress. Gradually adding small amounts each day is the key to sound speed improvement training. Trying to do too much too soon is a common cause of muscle-related injuries. Plan your program over a period of 3 to 6 months to maximize enjoyment and minimize pain and risk. Avoid using Step 7 (overspeed training) too soon. You need to train 2 to 3 weeks at three-quarter speed before moving into full speed sprinting and overspeed training to avoid muscle pulls.

6. *Alternate light and heavy days.* Many athletes make the mistake of trying to train hard every day. This is not recommended for several reasons. The body does not have adequate time to repair or rebuild itself, and the full benefit of your workout may not be realized. Also, injuries, boredom, and "peaking out" are much more likely with overtraining. It is advisable to alternate hard and easy days, to never overtrain on consecutive days, and to limit hard workouts to a maximum of

three per week. Overspeed training, weight training, and plyometric training are examples of strenuous programs that should be used no more than every other day. In fact, a maximum of four weight-training sessions, two plyometric sessions (never on the same day that a weight-training workout is scheduled), and three overspeed training sessions should be used weekly.

7. *Avoid the weekend-athlete approach to speed improvement.* One sure way to guarantee numerous injuries and illnesses is to train vigorously only on weekends. Use at least three workouts per week during your preseason speed improvement program.

8. *Pay close attention to your body signals.* Pain and other distress signals should not be ignored. Although some breathing discomfort and breathlessness is common and minor pain may be present in an ankle, foot, knee, hip, back, or other body part, pain that is severe, persistent, and especially sharp is a warning sign to stop exercising.

It is sound advice to stop exercising immediately if you notice any abnormal heart action (pulse irregularity, fluttering, palpitations in the chest or throat, or rapid heartbeats); pain or pressure in the middle of the chest, teeth, jaw, neck, or arm; dizziness; lightheadedness; or cold sweating or confusion.

9. *Master the proper form in your activity.* Proper running form is important to most fitness programs. Joggers should avoid running on the toes as this produces soreness in the calf muscles. The heel should strike the ground first before weight is rolled along the bottom of the foot to the toes for the push-off. The heel-to-toe movement involves initial contact with the heel, a quick weight transfer and roll forward, and a push-off with the toes. A number of other running-form problems often produce mild muscle and joint strain.

What general conditioning standards should be maintained in the preseason for football, basketball, and baseball players?

Because the preseason period should be used to improve speed, skill, and physical weaknesses, a general standard is often not maintained. Obviously, this is a mistake. The following standard requires a high degree of speed endurance, which is critical to football, basketball, and baseball:

	4-minute mile for men	**5-minute mile for women**
1. 2 × 880 yd	120 sec; 8-min rest interval between each repetition	150 sec; 8-min rest interval between each repetition
2. 4 × 440 yd	60 sec; 4-min rest interval between each repetition	75 sec; 4-min rest interval between each repetition
3. 8 × 220 yd	30 sec; 2-min rest interval between each repetition	37 sec; 2-min rest interval between each repetition

If you can meet one of these standards, you have a solid conditioning foundation and are ready to progress to an intense speed improvement program.

Does an innersole help reduce the shock waves created in sprinting?

Yes. Certain new types of protective pads appear to reduce the shock, prevent damage to the shock-absorbing system, and even permit activity while recovering from an injury. Viscoelastic polymers, made from synthetic compounds, closely resemble the body's cushioning system. The polymer has the properties of both elastic and fluid solids—the resilience of sponge rubber and the damping properties of fluids. Sorbothane is the best-known polymer on the market. A wedge of Sorbothane in the heel of a hard-soled walking shoe reduces the shock at the tibia by 50%. A full Sorbothane innersole may be more appropriate for running, tennis, and team sports. Shock waves through the body may be reduced by 50%–80% by using a polymer, and this reduced shock wave may prevent a number of solid-tissue and bone injuries.

What causes a stitch or pain in my side during a workout? Is this a danger sign?

The exact cause is a mystery. Pain occurs on either side of the chest, in the center of the chest and stomach, or in the liver area. It generally happens during severe exercise such as cross-country running, soccer, rugby, ice hockey, or basketball.

Because the pain occurs while the body is adjusting to the demands of exercise, it is believed to be caused by ischemia (insufficient supply of oxygen to a muscle) of the diaphragm or the rib muscles. It is interesting to note that ischemia of any muscle will cause pain. Another theory places the trouble at the site of the liver. It has been noted that pain often is relieved when an athlete bends over at the waist and presses hard in the area of the liver.

A stitch in the side is more common in the untrained athlete; it also occurs more frequently when one is exercising after a meal (circulatory adjustment at the beginning of exercise is slower in both instances). Do not stop at the first sign of pain. It will often disappear if you continue to exercise because the respiratory system catches up and adequate oxygen is supplied to the muscles. However, if severe pain persists, stop exercise and rest for 15 to 30 minutes. Train hard and warm up thoroughly and you may never experience a stitch in the side.

How is appendicitis distinguished from a common stitch in the side?

The difference is not easy to detect. A stitch in the side generally occurs during exercise, whereas appendix inflammation is more apt to be noticed while at rest. An inflamed appendix is usually acute in the teenage athlete, beginning with severe stomach pain and tenderness and rigidity on the right side. Other possible symptoms are nausea, vomiting, fever, and rapid pulse. Drawing the right leg toward the stomach provides some comfort.

If you suspect appendicitis, call a physician immediately, apply ice to the stomach, and administer no food, fluid, laxative, or heat. Do not panic at the first sign of these symptoms but let the physician make a diagnosis. People have undergone surgery because of simple gas pain.

Can most minor injuries be treated at home?

Most minor injuries can be managed through emergency and home treatment methods. There are four simple procedures of emergency treatment and initial home treatment for most muscle, ligament, and tendon strains; sprains, suspected fractures; bruises; and joint inflammation. This is the "RICE" method:

Rest. To prevent additional damage to injured tissue, stop exercising immediately. If the lower extremities are affected, secure a crutch to move about.

Ice. To decrease blood flow to the injured part and prevent swelling, apply ice immediately for 15 to 19 minutes (avoid direct ice contact with the skin).

Compression. To limit swelling, wrap a towel or bandage firmly around the ice and injured limb.

Elevation. To help drain excess fluid through gravity, raise the injured limb above the level of the heart.

Home treatment should begin as soon as possible. Continue to use the RICE method for at least 48 hours. On the fourth day, discontinue cold treatments and begin to apply moist or dry heat or sit in a whirlpool twice daily for 15 to 30 minutes. Depending on the severity of the injury, mild exercise can resume on the fourth or fifth day.

What is the proper way to use ice therapy in the treatment of injuries?

Ice therapy (cryotherapy) can be used immediately following an injury (for 2 to 4 days) and during the rehabilitation phase of treatment (after 4 days).

Immediately following an injury, ice relieves pain by impeding the conduction of pain messages along the smaller, slow-conducting nerve fibers by stimulating the production of endorphins and by preventing pain messages from reaching the brain. Cold also limits swelling, blood clot formation, and tissue damage in the first 9 to 16 minutes of application. Less blood flows through constricted arteries, and thus temperature is decreased, reducing the metabolic requirements of the injured part.

Follow these basic suggestions when using ice therapy on a soft-tissue injury:

- Apply ice immediately after any injury that may cause swelling.
- Apply some form of light pressure (bandage) and elevate the injured part.
- After the area is cold, stretch the injured part carefully and slowly until pain occurs.
- Apply ice for no longer than 19 minutes at a time and reapply for 19 minutes every hour for 4 hours.
- Avoid applying ice directly to the tissue unless an ice massage is being used. Place ice cubes in a plastic bag under a tensor bandage or fill Styrofoam cups with water and freeze them. Wait until the surface of the cup melts before applying it to the skin. Additional methods include ice water, rubber ice packs, instant cold chemical packs, snow, and freeze spray.

How is a muscle cramp relieved?

A cramp can be relieved by stretching the involved muscle. To relieve a cramp in the back of the lower leg, assume a seated position with the leg fully extended. Instruct someone to apply steady pressure on the ball of the foot. If you are alone, place a towel around the toe of the shoe and pull steadily for several minutes while the leg is fully extended. For a cramp in the front of the upper leg (quadricep group), stand on the opposite leg, bend the knee backward, then grasp the ankle and pull it toward your buttocks. To relieve a cramp in the back of the upper leg (hamstring group), fully extend the knee and flex the hip. A very firm massage is also helpful in some cases.

What causes a muscle cramp?

The exact cause is unknown. A cramp appears to be a result of a muscle's shortening too much (contraction of any muscle causes shortening). It could also occur from a rigorous muscle contraction that takes place when the muscle is already partially shortened. Low levels of salt, potassium, and magnesium also increase the possibility of a cramp.

The much-feared stomach cramp during swimming rarely occurs. One investigation failed to find a single case of stomach cramp in the 30,000 swimmers who were studied.

In most athletes, cramps can be prevented by

- using static flexibility exercises (steady pressure at maximum range of movement) instead of bouncing hard;
- avoiding jerky movements until properly warmed up;
- using a 10- to 15-minute warm-up period;
- drinking plenty of water before, during, and after practice (fatigue is also delayed with water intake); and
- eating more fruits and vegetables.

Severe cramps in the back of the lower leg, in the back of the upper leg, and in the front of the upper leg are common in sports.

NASE Complete Speed Test Battery

All the endless diversity of the external manifestations of the activity of the brain can be finally regarded as one phenomenon—that of muscular movement.
—Sechenov

NASE Complete Speed Test Battery

Tests	Procedures
Stationary 40-yd dash	Subject assumes a 3-point football or a track stance and responds to the commands "Get set, go." Timer is located at the finish line and starts the watch on the command "Go." The watch can also be started on a visual signal such as the dropping of an arm. The command "Go" is given or a football (hand) is moved on the ground.
Stationary self 40-, 80-, 120-yd dash	Subject begins when ready. One timer starts a stopwatch on the first movement of the athlete and stops it when the runner trips a flag draped over the finish tape at the 40-yd mark. A second timer starts a stopwatch at the 40-yd mark and stops it when the runner trips a flag draped over the tape at the 80-yd mark. A third timer starts a stopwatch at the 80-yd mark and stops it when the runner trips a flag draped over the tape at the 120-yd mark.
Flying 40-yd dash	The above time from the 40- to the 80-yd mark is used as the flying 40-yd time.

Acceleration	Subtract the flying 40-yd time from the stationary self 40-yd time.
Speed endurance	Compare the flying 40 time above with the time from the 80- to the 120-yd tape. The difference between the two scores is your speed endurance.
Stride length	Two markers are placed 25 yd apart on a smooth surface approximately 50 yd from the starting line. Runner reaches maximum speed prior to reaching the 25-yd area. Stride length is measured from the tip of the rear toe to the tip of the front toe and recorded to the nearest inch.
Stride rate	This can be calculated from flying 40-yd time and stride length: 1,440 in. (40 yd) ÷ stride length (in.) ÷ flying 40-yd time = stride rate (steps per sec) or by using the stride rate matrix in Table 2.3.
Standing triple jump	In the standing long jump position, subject jumps forward (two-foot takeoff) as far as possible, landing on only one foot before immediately jumping to the opposite foot, taking one final jump, and landing on both feet (same as running triple except for takeoff).
Vertical jump	A two-foot takeoff is performed from a standing position near a wall. Distance is measured from the highest reaching point with feet flat on the ground to the highest point touched during the jump.
Leg power balance	Right-/left-leg hop: With a 15-yd flying start, subject begins a one-legged hop at the starting tape and continues hopping 20 yd to the finish tape. Flags are used on start and finish tapes as in the flying 40-yd dash.
Total body strength	Clean: The maximum weight lifted from the ground to the shoulders is recorded in pounds.
Leg strength (static)	Subject stands erect in foot-placement markings grasping the bar with the palms down. Knees are bent to 119° and the back is straight. The chain is connected to the dynanometer, the belt tight-

ened, and the subject instructed to pull upward with both arms at the same time he or she attempts to straighten the legs. The best of three attempts is recorded in pounds.

Leg strength (dynamic)

The seat on a Universal, Nautilus, or similar leg press station or free weight (squat) is adjusted until the legs are at right angles. The object is to locate each subject's 1 RM (maximum lift for 1 repetition) and record that lift in pounds.

Arm/shoulder pushing strength

Bench press: Using the overhand grip while lying on the back on a bench or floor with both knees raised, subject performs one repetition of the bench press by lowering the bar to the chest and pressing it back to the starting position. The maximum amount of weight lifted is recorded in pounds.

Dip (20-sec): Subject grasps the parallel bars with the arms straight. The body is lowered until the shoulders are below the elbows, then returned to the upright position with both arms extended. No excessive swinging is permitted. The number of correct repetitions in 20 sec is recorded.

Chin (20 sec): Subject grasps bar, palms away, while in a hanging, straight-arm position. The body is pulled up until the chin is over the bar, then returned to the straight-arm hanging position. No excess swinging is permitted. The number of correct repetitions performed in 20 sec is recorded.

Abdominals

Sit-ups: Lying on back, knees bent to right angles, hands behind the head, subject sits up, bringing elbows to the knees as often as possible in 60 sec. The total number of correct repetitions is recorded.

Flexibility

Subject sits on the floor with knees together and feet flat against the measuring bench. Subjects reach forward slowly with arms extended and knees locked. The number of inches the subject reaches past the toes is recorded.

Body fat

Skinfold calipers are used to measure sites at the back of the arm and iliac crest for women and at the back of the arm, stomach, and chest for men.

Back of upper arm: Midway between the elbow and the tip of the shoulder, the skin and fatty tissue are pinched using the index finger and thumb to lift upward. Calipers are placed 1/16 in. below the pinch.

Iliac crest: The diagonal fold on the top of the right or left hip is pinched and measured as described above.

Stomach: A deep horizontal pinch is taken about 1 in. to the right of the navel.

Chest: Pinch the skin about 1 in. to the right of the right nipple.

Anaerobic capacity

Complete 2 laps on a standard .25 mi track or measure off 880 yd on a 400-m track and run that distance as fast as possible.

Aerobic capacity

Complete 6 laps on a standard .25-mi track or measure off 1.5 mi on a 400-m track and run that distance as fast as possible.

Reaction time

Subtract your 40-yd-dash time determined with a starter from your 40-yd-dash self-start time. The difference is recorded to the nearest 0.1 sec.

Appendix C

Recording Progress

Make haste: the better foot before.
—William Shakespeare

Your Speed Profile

Name _____ Birthdate _____

Sport(s) and position _____

Test weakness areas:

Test	Date	Initial test scores	1 month later	3 months later	5 months later
Stationary 40					
NASE 40					
Flying 40					
Acceleration					
80–120					
Speed endurance					
Stride rate					
Stride length					
Leg press					
Leg extension (quadricep)					

Test	Date	Initial test scores	1 month later	3 months later	5 months later
Leg curl (hamstring)					
Standing triple					
Vertical jump					
Height					
Weight					

ABOUT THE AUTHORS

 Dr. George B. Dintiman is internationally known for his work in speed improvement. He is the president of the National Association of Speed and Explosion (NASE) as well as the editor of its monthly magazine, SPORTSPEED. His book, *How to Run Faster*, is world-renowned, and its program of speed improvement is used by professional and amateur athletes throughout the world.

Due to his strong affiliation with the NASE, Dr. Dintiman hosts a national network of speed clinics and camps for athletes of all ages and skill levels. In addition, he is a professor of health and physical education at Virginia Commonwealth University and enjoys tennis, road racing, and writing.

 With a PED from Indiana University and 25 years experience as a coach and athlete, Bob Ward is highly regarded by many professional, college, high school, and Olympic teams for his vast knowledge and expertise in the area of sport conditioning. Presently, he is the conditioning coach for the Dallas Cowboys Football Club.

Dr. Ward became aware of the need for sport conditioning while competing as an athlete in football and track. He has coached several Olympic champions and numerous championship football and track teams. During his tenure at Fullerton College, athletes he coached set national records in the high hurdle relay, the discus, and the hammer throw.

Both authors are founders of the NASE and are internationally known lecturers and speed consultants. Dr. Dintiman is the author of 18 books on sports, health, fitness, nutrition, weight control, and disease prevention. Dr. Ward has authored other books on sportspeed and lectured extensively on conditioning, track and field, and nutritional support for athletes.